The Greatest Stories Ever Told (About Baseball)

OTHER BOOKS BY KEVIN NELSON

Baseball's Greatest Quotes
Baseball's Greatest Insults

The Greatest Stories Ever Told (About Baseball)

KEVIN NELSON

Illustrations by Sheila Nelson

A Perigee Book

Perigee Books
are published by
The Putnam Publishing Group
200 Madison Avenue
New York, NY 10016

Library of Congress Cataloging-in-Publication Data

Nelson, Kevin, date.
The greatest stories ever told (about baseball)

1. Baseball—United States—Addresses, essays,
lectures.   I. Title.
GV863.A1N45   1986   796.357′0973   85-25871
ISBN 0-399-51227-6

Printed in the United States of America

1   2   3   4   5   6   7   8   9   10

For my mother,
with love

Contents

Preface

"Baseball isn't statistics. Baseball is DiMaggio rounding second."

—JIMMY CANNON

To be blunt, numbers bore me. Would it be heresy to confess that, though I've sat in on hundreds of baseball games in my life, I've never once bothered to keep a scorecard of a game in progress? Here, *you* can do the scribbling; let me yell until I'm hoarse, argue with the guy in front of me, eat peanuts, guzzle beer, run back and forth to the men's room, watch the girls, stretch out in the sun and bake, all the while keeping one heavy-lidded eye on the proceedings on the field. Now that's baseball!

There are those who would argue, of course, that by neglecting the numbers I am missing an essential element of the game. They may be right. But I say those people—baseball accountants who bury their heads in the statistical arcana of the game, who concentrate on its mathematical infrastructure, who cannot appreciate a play in the field without first relating it to the record books—are often blind to the simple, unclouded beauty and joy and magic of the sport. That is, DiMaggio rounding second.

For me, the greatest charm of baseball is its stories, its good humor, its tall tales. While the pitcher is taking his warm-up tosses, who would rather not hear a good joke about Reggie Jackson than a recitation of his power-hitting stats? (You may choose the latter, but don't sit next to me.) It's no accident that men such as Tommy Lasorda, Ron Luciano and Bob Uecker are in demand on the banquet circuit. They're storytellers. They say things that make people laugh.

Statistics are more for private consumption and contemplation, while a good story, well-told, is a public craft. Like an outdoor sculpture, it can be enjoyed and shared by everyone. A good story, unlike a stat, can be appreciated even by those who care nothing or know nothing about baseball; it reaches out and includes, it draws people in, establishes common ground. Baseball anecdotalists—the legend-spinners—are thought by many to be an amusing, idiosyncratic sidelight to the game. On the contrary, they are at the very heart of its appeal. Where would Troy be without Homer?

In the manner of myth, great baseball stories are handed down from generation to generation and form a bond between young and old, underlining and strengthening our connections as a people, our essential unity, despite the potential divisiveness of the moment. If nothing else, we Americans have baseball in common. I never saw Ted Williams on a ball field, but because of the stories I've heard and the legends that have grown up around him, he seems in some ways as close to me as the stars in the game today. Ted Williams serves as a meeting ground, a starting point from which my father's generation can speak to my own. In turn, I can relate stories of Mike Schmidt and Tom Seaver (through this book, in fact) to kids who will never see them play.

In this way baseball resembles a giant ball of string. Its stories under- and overlap and break off and pick up in a different place and go round and round again. Each successive generation adds new threads to the ball—a daring baserunning gambit by Tim Raines, a monstrous Dwight Gooden performance—just as the old yarns are altered or embellished according to the demands of the time. Very little is forgotten. In baseball, more so than any other sport, the past is a living thing; it informs the present (Is Dale

Murphy the new Babe Ruth?) and establishes the criteria for which future players will be judged (Is Joe Phenom the next Dale Murphy?). Old tales are woven into new tales; new tales are created and added, and the already complex, textured fabric of baseball lore grows richer.

Ordinarily, such a wonderful, perpetually renewing body of stories—both oral and written—would indicate a healthy interest in a game that, despite strikes and cocaine, is very much alive and kicking. It's easy to forget that essential fact, though. Faced with the wave upon wave of statistical analyses, prognostications, scouting reports, commentaries, elegiac tributes (Ah, spring!), reminiscences, interviews, books, histories, documentaries and TV specials that roll in every spring and continue unabated until late October, the typical fan cannot be blamed for shouting, "Enough, already!"

Do we really need all this hype? It might be easier to fathom if so much of it didn't revolve around the same subject: money. All of us are tired of reading about salaries. Okay, okay, ballplayers make some real coin. And they're ungrateful wretches, to boot. Professional baseball is an industry, to be sure, but can't we talk about something else for a while?

You will find almost nothing in this book concerning contract negotiations, strikes, power squabbles between players and owners, labor-management relations, etc. And you will find precious little about owners here. Owners do not play the game; they only screw it up. My focus is on the men, past and present, who play the game on the field. Anyone wearing a suit and tie, I regard with suspicion.

Another thing I regard with suspicion is statistics. (You may have noticed.) Of course numbers can be entertaining and enlightening. In many ways they do form, in Roger Angell's words, "the critical dimensions of the game." But what bothers me is the cult that has sprung up around them. Statistics-worshipers influence so much of baseball "thinking" these days (the word is used loosely). And I'm not referring to scouts or managers; I'm talking about the reductionists who think they can determine a ballplayer's, or a team's, performance based on pseudoscientific formulae which only they and their fellow cultists can ever hope to understand. This is reading tea leaves, folks. Believe it at your peril.

The best statistical forecasters/analysts tend, like any ordinary Joe on the street, to place too much weight on the favorites, underestimate the underdogs, miss the sleepers and be surprised, even shocked, by unexpected developments. And when the final reckoning must be made, when all the statistical detritus has been piled up to the sky, they find they must rely on that most human, most unmathematical of concepts—their own hunches. This is a fitting irony, though one that the statistical Stalinists probably will not appreciate.

Though admittedly numbers have informed many of the opinions expressed herein, readers of this volume are mostly safe from statistics. I keep them out of sight, where they properly belong. My purpose is to take a fresh look at some of the game's myths—break up the cobwebs, open the windows, get a broom in there and do some spring cleaning, if you will, in our national pastime's attic. We are so familiar with some of the best-known names (Willie Mays, Casey Stengel, Satchel Paige, et al.) that we may have come to take them for granted. That should never be allowed to happen. These men are a national treasure, a vital and vivid part of our history and our dream-lives.

This is a more personal work than the title, *The Greatest Stories Ever Told (About Baseball)*, would suggest. Some of these stories aren't great at all; rather, they simply struck me as funny, or compelling in some way, or deserving of more attention than they have generally received. No doubt one or two of your favorite superheroes have been left out. This book is not intended to be encyclopedic; it plays favorites and holds opinions, informed or otherwise. Nor will you necessarily find rounded portraits of these ballplayers. This is history through the back door, anecdotal rather than biographical, written to enhance your enjoyment and appreciation of the game.

One final point. Many writers, when recalling a favored piece of baseball lore, will preface the stories with the phrase, "It's probably apocryphal, but . . ." You won't find that sort of defensiveness in this book. I make no apologies for apocrypha; indeed, I have come to praise it, salute it, revel in it. Baseball is founded on a myth—Abner Doubleday and Cooperstown—and it is, as Richard Adams wrote, "the bright and inexhaustible ring of myth" that breathes life into the old game and renders, at end, the businessmen and accountants of baseball impotent.

Some great stories, such as Babe Ruth hitting a home run into the bleachers at Wrigley Field after pointing to the spot, may not have happened—but so what? As others have pointed out, just because a thing happened doesn't make it true. By the same token, just because it didn't happen doesn't make it false. Myth sticks around—lives!—because it speaks to the permanent, essential part of ourselves, our being. A man with the audacity to call his home run shot, and then *do* it, touches something universal in us all, and we need not feel embarrassed about it.

—Kevin Nelson
Walnut Creek, California

1
Batter Up! The Greatest of Them All

"The more I see of Babe, the more he seems a figure out of mythology."

—A BOSTON SPORTSWRITER, 1918

1

EVERYTHING about Babe Ruth was great, especially his home runs. The longest home run he ever hit may be the longest home run ever hit—anywhere, anytime, by anybody. Nobody had ever seen anything quite like it. The ball traveled, on the fly, around six hundred feet, well over the low right-center field fence and onto a horse-racing track that encircled the field. The game, the opener of the 1919 spring season, was at Tampa's old Plant Field, in the fairgrounds. Later they erected a plaque at the site entitled BABE'S LONGEST HOMER. It described how "4,300 screaming fans" witnessed the historic act, including "famed evangelist Billy Sunday, an ex–major leaguer himself, who was conducting a tent revival on the Florida Fair grounds nearby."

Ruth was twenty-four at the time, and had not joined the Yankees yet. Still a member of the Red Sox, he was pitching and playing the outfield only part-time. The debate over whether he should remain a pitcher or become a full-time hitter was still being argued, though the issue would've been settled by acclamation if the fans had had the final say.

They wanted to see Ruth hit. They paid to see him hit. He swung the bat and got results like no man they had ever seen. In the World Series the year before, a cocky, showboating Ruth had hit the first ball pitched to him in batting practice over the wall in Wrigley Field. In a game in Washington he hit a ball out of the park that landed in somebody's garden and scared their dog. Truly, this was a man who could frighten anyone with his bat, man or beast.

Ruth had come to training camp that year demanding that the Red Sox management make up its mind—either pitch him or play him in the outfield. No more switching back and forth. The Babe himself wanted to play every day. He saw how people reacted to his home runs and he wondered what might happen if he concentrated on his hitting alone.

Consider what this meant. Hall of Famers Walter Johnson and Christy Mathewson are widely considered to be the finest pitchers of this era, and Ruth was their equal. He outdueled Johnson on numerous occasions, and had snapped Mathewson's long-standing record for consecutive shutout innings in World Series play. If there had been a Cy Young Award in 1916, Ruth would have won it. He dominated American League hitters that year and again the next season, confirming his status as one of the very best pitchers in all of baseball.

Many believe he could've made the Hall of Fame solely on his pitching. Tris Speaker, the gifted center fielder, thought Ruth was a fool to forsake pitching for the hardships of everyday duty. "Ruth made a grave mistake when he gave up pitching," Speaker said. "Working once a week, he might've lasted a long time and become a great star." Such sentiments, however ridiculous they may appear today, were shared by many baseball experts of the time. Smokey Joe Wood had moved from pitching to the outfield, but only because an arm injury forced him to do it. Ruth's switch was something different. It was a wholly preposterous act. Put in modern terms, it would be like a young Tom Seaver, coming off his best season with the Mets, wanting to chuck it all to see if he could become Reggie Jackson.

And many onlookers were rooting against him. They did not want to see Ruth do it, they wanted to see the big ape fall flat on his face. Baseball was, everyone knew, an extremely difficult sport, requiring the utmost in reflexes, concentration and athletic ability. Yet here was a big, goofy-looking man-child who wanted to go from being the game's best pitcher to being its best hitter. After excelling on the mound, after dominating a craft that others took a lifetime to learn, he was going to step away from it and try to master an entirely different discipline. Baseball was not so tough, Babe Ruth seemed to say. Any kid could do it.

Before his death Casey Stengel used to tell the story of the first time he ever saw Ruth play. They were in a game against each other. A minor leaguer and unknown at the time, Ruth hit a deep fly into right that Stengel, then in his early twenties and an outfielder with excellent foot speed, barely shagged down. When Casey returned to the dugout after the inning, his teammates razzed him for almost letting a kid hit a ball over his head. So, the next time the kid came up, Stengel moved back some twenty-five feet in the fenceless outfield pasture, confident he was safe. Ruth creamed a pitch over Stengel for a triple.

Ross Youngs, the Hall of Fame outfielder who was playing in right for the Giants that day in Tampa, must've felt like Casey did. There was no chance on the ball Ruth hit over his head. Turning and running with the crack of the bat, Youngs followed the flight of the ball as it rose in the sky. Then, knowing it was hopeless, he stopped running and, like Billy Sunday and the thousands of others who may have felt they were witnessing a miracle, stood and watched in amazement. The ball kept going and going and going.

2

Babe Ruth was a prodigious lover and an even bigger eater; he chewed tobacco and gum constantly, dipped snuff, smoked cigars and cigarettes, drove big, flashy cars and spent money like a millionaire, wore a camel's hair coat and promised to hit home runs for sick kids in the hospital; he dug jazz; he marveled at the power of trains and when a young boy he rode up and down elevators for fun; he loved to wrestle and play practical jokes, ate fifteen-egg omelettes and six hot dogs at a sitting, drank enormously and often, loved to carouse late at night and hit all the happening clubs, was crude and charming and a show-off; he made lots of money and tipped outrageously; he gambled on the horses; he loved kids and animals, had two wives and scores of sexual liaisons in his lifetime, and sometimes satisfied two or three women in a night.

Most of all, though, Babe Ruth was a home run hitter. No one could touch him then—and no one can touch him now—when it came to hitting baseballs over great distances with such awesome regularity. In Chicago, in Boston, in the old Polo Grounds in New York City, almost wherever he went, in whatever stadium he played, he hit the longest ball that anyone watching at the time had ever seen hit. The stupendous was, for Ruth, ordinary. He once hit a home run into Narragansett Bay. A homer of his in St. Louis sailed out of the park and broke the front window of a home on the other side of the street. Angry at himself for striking out, he broke his bat—in one stroke—by banging it against the ground. He hit pop flies so high nobody could catch them. In an exhibition at Wrigley Field, facing an array of pitchers, he hit over a hundred balls into the seats in an hour. Besides his famous homer against Charlie Root in the '32 Series, there are a number of other instances in which Ruth called his shot in a ball game. One time he waved the right fielder for the opposing team back as he approached the batter's box. Noticing that the guy hadn't moved despite his instructions, Ruth hit a line shot over his head. The left field wall at Chattanooga's Engel Stadium is a formidable three hundred sixty-eight feet down the line and forty feet high. Out in center, the fence stands twenty-five feet high and some four hundred twenty feet from home plate. Here, in this most Brobdingnagian of minor league parks, Ruth also claims honors for the ball hit farthest: a homer over the right-center field fence that cleared the stadium and landed in an open coal car heading west. After a roundabout trip through the South, the ball was later picked up in St. Louis, Missouri, and some wits claim that *that* ball—with a traveling distance of two thousand miles or so—was really the longest home run of all time.

3

Oddly, perhaps, the absence for the most part of moving pictures to record his acts has not diminished our awe of Ruth over time; rather it seems to have deepened it. The stories that have come down about the man, the accounts of what he did on a ball field, seem composed partly of fact and partly of some other substance that we can't quite define yet compels us nevertheless.

People these days tend to think of Ruth as he was toward the end of his career, fat and slow, with a bulging stomach and little broomstick legs that looked like they might break under the weight they were forced to carry. The Babe as a young man presents a far different picture. He was lithe and rangy as a halfback. His powerful thighs anchored a formidable torso that, together with his strong arms and wrists, formed what Yankee teammate Pete Appleton called "the prettiest swing of all." In a day when it was rare to see someone over six feet, he stood six-foot-two. His playing weight was a solid one hundred eighty pounds, and only in the later years did it balloon over two hundred twenty.

Ruth was no one-dimensional freak, as is sometimes charged. He did not play in an American League in which pitchers don't hit and hitters don't field. He could run and go get 'em in the outfield, and he could throw too. By all the traditional measurements he was as good an all-around player as ever stepped on a ball field, and at his best he attained, as Roger Angell wrote about Roberto Clemente just before his death, "something close to the level of absolute perfection, playing to win but also playing the game almost as if it were a form of punishment for everyone else on the field."

It need not be established that Ruth was the greatest of all time in order to appreciate what he did for baseball. He was its great alchemist. He virtually invented the home run as an act of stunning significance in a baseball game. And, in so doing, transformed the game on the field and made it into something that it was not before. What was assumed before Ruth could not be assumed after him. The old rules no longer applied. He led baseball through a revolution that brought down the old structure of things and laid the foundation for the game we see today.

Back then, very few players held the bat at the end when they hit. Most everybody choked up, hoping only to meet the ball and chip out a single or move the runners on base along. This was "inside baseball"—scratch and claw and bite for those two or three runs and then play tight defense and hope your pitching held. Ty Cobb was the prototype player of this style of ball: a line-drive, singles-type hitter and a slashing baserunner. Though there are of course many in the game who still belong to this school—as a team, the Willie McGee and Vince Coleman–led St. Louis Cardinals are inside baseballers—what's important to understand is that before 1920 there were no alternatives. Anyone who knew anything at all about baseball played it the scratch-and-claw way. Inside baseball was an orthodoxy of such power that it made people blind. They could not see how the game could be played any other way.

Then along came Ruth. Swinging a forty-two-ounce bat and holding it at the end, he exploded the orthodoxies. He exposed the decrepit thinking behind them and demonstrated a new way of doing things that featured the home run as centerpiece. It's a noteworthy coincidence that as Ruth's powers and fame grew, Cobb's influence declined. Ruth represented the new age, Cobb the old.

One could easily argue that Babe Ruth invented the modern game of baseball. Every player who takes the field today owes a debt to him. Dale Murphy and Pedro Guerrero, guys like that, might've had to learn to bunt if it weren't for Ruth. Red Smith wrote, "He changed the rules, the equipment and the strategy of baseball. Reasoning that if one Babe Ruth could fill a park, sixteen would fill all the parks, the owners instructed the manufacturers to produce a livelier ball that would make every man a home run king." Earl Weaver, one of the most successful present-day managers, may also be the leading proponent of the baseball philosophy first enunciated by Ruth. "Strategy in baseball is overrated," Earl has said. "People say, 'That Weaver, he plays for the long ball too much.' You bet I do. Hit 'em out. Then I got no worry about somebody lousing up a bunt, I got no worry about the hit-and-run. Just instant runs. You bet Weaver likes the long ball."

An early antagonist of Ruth's, and the chief theoretical spokesman for inside baseball, was John McGraw, the manager of the New York Giants whose nickname of "Little Napoleon" derived from his deft use of tactics and strategy to win games. McGraw not only went by the book, he wrote most of it. He believed firmly in such devices as the hit-and-run and the squeeze play, and the force of his personality and his success as a leader made his Giants the most famous and admired team in the era before and just after World War I.

To the puppetmaster McGraw, Babe Ruth was a crude and unsophisticated character, the proverbial bull in a china shop. McGraw once scoffed that if Ruth kept swinging from the heels like he did, he'd ground into a hundred double plays in a season. The Babe never forgot this comment. Every time in spring ball he hit a homer against the Giants, he'd yell at McGraw in the dugout, "How's that for a double play, Mac?"

But Little Napoleon was no easy mark. He never went down without a fight, and he seldom went down at all. For two years running, McGraw's Giants beat Ruth's Yankees to claim the baseball title of New York City and the world. In their battle, Mr. Inside Baseball was beating the stuffing out of Mr. Out-of-the-Park.

The third straight all–New York World Series occurred in 1923, only this one had a different ending than the previous two. In game two Ruth hit two crushing back-to-back homers, the first of which was described by Heywood Broun: "The ball started climbing from the moment it left the plate. It was a pop fly with a brand new gland and, although it flew high, it also flew far." Broun added, "We wonder whether new baseballs conversing in the original package ever remark: 'Join Ruth and see the world.'" The Yankees at last beat McGraw and, in the process, a number of baseballs got a chance to see the world. With Ruth foremost among them, players on both sides rocked the crowds with their homers and power hitting—yet another indication that the inside game was out, and no longer reigned supreme in the land. Little Napoleon had had his Waterloo.

4

When a player goes after a record, it's a given that he has something to shoot for, a goal. Like a mountaineer with his eyes set on the peak he is climbing, this goal energizes and motivates him and keeps him going despite all the hardships. His goal is to break the record, and he won't stop until he does it.

After he achieves his goal, however, changes occur both in the challenger's mind and in the new physical reality he must face. He is no longer chasing the record; he *is* the record holder. The goal that he has sought for so long has been displaced; what is ahead of him now is less clear, less certain. There are no more records to break, no more goals to fasten on, unless he creates them in his own mind. *Nobody has ever been out there but me.* Inevitably, out of fatigue or relief or simple boredom, the new record holder begins to slow his advance and, in some cases, to stop. Look at Rickey Henderson chasing Lou Brock. Or Brock chasing Maury Wills before that. Or Henry Aaron busting Ruth's career homer mark. They all slowed down after they got what they were after. They had their records.

Consider, then, what Babe Ruth did. When he entered the game the home run was as rare as a good drink in Salt Lake City. Practically nobody hit them. If you hit as many as ten in a season, you belonged in the primate cage at the zoo. When, in his first season as a full-time player, Ruth hit twenty-nine, it was an astounding, unheard of feat that ranked just below the construction of the Cheops Pyramid. The next season, he nearly doubled that figure.

The numbers clatter on, the most impressive being this one: Before him the all-time career home run mark was one hundred thirty-seven, and Ruth surpassed that in 1921, in only his second year as a Yankee. In other words, every home run he hit after that point broke his own record. From a career perspective, the only home run goals he had to beat were of his own making—unlike Henry Aaron, he had nobody out there to lead the way, to cut a path for him. With every swing of his bat he was pushing out the limits of what was possible, extending the boundaries of what was known. "Thus," writes the mythologist Joseph Campbell in *A Hero with a Thousand Faces,* "the sailors of the bold vessels of

Columbus, breaking the horizon of the medieval mind, had to be cozened and urged on by example, because of their fear of the fabled leviathans, mermaids, dragon kings, and other monsters of the deep." Ruth, leading by example, discovered the place, and the ships captained by Foxx and Gehrig and Greenberg—and later still, Mays and Aaron and Mantle—came after.

5

For anyone writing about Ruth, or for those who remember him and saw him play, there is a natural tendency to bury him in hyperbole. The Best! The Greatest! The One and Only! You never saw anything like it! Quite understandably, the more skeptical modern reader tends to regard these accounts with suspicion.

Though a more restrained approach to Ruth might be advisable, it's not all that easy to muster. His exploits, on and off the field, encouraged hyperbole. It was said he never changed his underpants. He once ate a straw hat. He could drive a golf ball more than three hundred fifty yards. He could drink any three men under the table. Suffering from a hangover in spring training, he collided with a palm tree while chasing a fly ball. How does one maintain a moderate stance when talking about this immoderate, gloriously excessive man?

Ruth's nature was outgoing, demanding, egocentric, fulsome, petulant, gracious, extraordinarily giving and all-embracing, whiny, boastful, proud, sweet, sentimental, corny, crass and loving. To Ruth, as to a child, the world revolved around himself. After World War I, General Ferdinand Foch, the French field marshal who was one of the leaders of the Allied effort, headed a ticker tape parade down Broadway. There to greet the seventy-year-old General was the Babe, who said to him, "Hey Gen, they tell me you were in the war."

His behavior seemed spontaneous and instinctual, as if emanating from powerful, hidden sources. "He was like a damn animal," Rube Bressler, the old-time pitcher, said. "He had that instinct. They know when it's going to rain, things like that. Nature, that was Ruth!" Yes! That was Ruth! Put an exclamation point after his name. He deserves it. For he lived life grandly, in the manner of a man who knows he is blessed and need not fear. One morning, for kicks, he put down a twenty-dollar tip on a coffee-and-eggs breakfast tab just to see what reaction he'd get from the waiter who, to Ruth's shock, said nothing about it. As he was about to leave, Ruth couldn't hold back any longer. He grabbed the waiter by the collar, saying, "Hey buster, ain't that the biggest tip you ever had?" "No," said the waiter. "Yesterday I served you coffee and toast and you gave me a thirty-dollar tip."

Another glimpse into the Ruth personality is provided by Robert Creamer in his superb biography of him. Ruth, one of the most famous men in America in the twenties, was of course invited to any number of parties and society functions where he met and mingled with the wealthiest and most successful people in the country. At one particular function, a formal dinner party, they served an asparagus salad. Not sure which was the proper fork to use, Ruth waited until the others had started before trying the salad. His first taste wasn't good, so he put down his fork and delicately pushed the plate away.

"Don't you care for the salad, Mr. Ruth?" the hostess asked.

"Oh, it's not that," he answered politely. "It's just that asparagus makes my urine smell."

6

Beyond the numbers he rolled up, which are impressive enough, there was something about the way Babe Ruth hit those long home run balls that was utterly unique and astonishing. His was not a triumph only of quantity, but of quality too. Think of what it's like to watch Jim Rice or Eddie Murray at the plate today—that feeling you have, in

Updike's phrase, "that crowds the throat with joy"—and you get a sense of how lucky a person was to have seen Ruth. He was never a cheap pitty-pat hitter in the fashion of the day; always, he swung for the fences. The force of his swing was prodigious and sometimes after a cut his body would twist all the way around in a full circle, à la Reggie Jackson. "When Ruth misses a swipe at the ball, the stands quiver," an observer wrote in that familiar, hyperbolic tone of the time.

Red Smith wrote, "Crowds were to Ruth as water to a fish." The fans loved him, and Ruth played to them like the natural-born showman he was. What the people wanted, he gave them. More than once he had to be carried off the field on a stretcher after an injury (feigned or no). Then he would dramatically return to the lineup the next day and explode with a shower of home runs. "What was it like pitching to him? Like looking into a lion's jaw, that's what," Wes Ferrell told Donald Honig. "Hell, man, you're pitching to a *legend*! And you knew, too, that if he hits a home run, he's gonna get the cheers, and if he strikes out, he's still gonna get the cheers. You were *nothing* out there when Ruth came up." Fans cheered as Ruth stepped toward home plate to bat, and they heckled the outfielders for playing him so deep. It was a disappointment whenever Ruth didn't hit one out in a game, and the Babe never wanted to disappoint anybody on a ball field.

He had a flair for the appropriate. He hit the first home run in All-Star competition. Like an emperor bestowing gifts to the far provinces, he was the first to hit a homer in every American League city he visited. One year Red Sox infielder Fred Haney hit a home run against the Yankees, one of the very few in his career. As he walked past Ruth afterward, he said, "You're only forty-six ahead of me now, Babe." On his next at bat Ruth hit a towering home run far over the center field wall. As he passed Haney at third base while rounding the bases, Babe said, "How do we stand now, kid?"

When they opened Yankee Stadium, the Chartres of baseball, Ruth christened it with a homer. During the Sec-

ond World War, in a benefit game at the Stadium, he hit a
long foul into the right field seats which, ever the ham, he
treated as a home run, trotting around the bases to the ap-
plause of the crowd. In the mid-thirties, after being released
by the Yankees, he went over to the Boston Braves and
then, in a kind of goodbye to baseball, hit three massive
home runs in a game in Forbes Field in Pittsburgh. Lloyd
Waner, playing the outfield for the Pirates that day, said one
of the home runs looked like "it had a little engine in it."

After less than thirty games with the Braves, Ruth quit.
And his days as a player were over. He died of cancer in
1948, in a New York City hospital. Only hours before his
death a nurse reportedly found Ruth, ravaged and wasted by
the disease, crawling across the hospital room floor. The
horrified nurse asked Ruth what he was doing and he said,
"I'm entering the Valley." If the Babe ever did make it to
that Valley, chances are he could have hit a ball across it.

2
Tall Tales and Titans

"The years go on, the years slip by,
The heroes rise, the heroes die,
There'll come a day, not far away,
A day of fans that knew not Ty."

—ANONYMOUS

Fables

1

THE GAME IS IN Pittsburgh, sometime in the early 1900s. The opponent: unknown. At shortstop for the Pirates is the multitalented Honus Wagner who, it was said, "walks like a crab, plays like an octopus, and hits like the devil."

A ground ball is hit toward Wagner. At the same time a rabbit emerges from a hole in the base of the grandstands and races across the infield. Wagner doesn't hesitate for a second, scooping up the rabbit in his glove and throwing it to first.

Says Wagner with a satisfied grin, "I got the runner by a hare."

2

We'll let Leo Durocher tell this one:

"It's spring training, you see, not too many people around. I'm sitting by myself in the dugout, and a horse trots up to me and says he wants to play for the Dodgers. He's not a bad-looking nag, so I say, 'Okay, show me what you got.'

"I go out to the mound and throw a couple to him. Nothin' too tough, I don't wanna embarrass the nag. So the horse takes a bat in his teeth and hits two or three into the stands.

"He's smiling pretty good after that, so I say to him, 'Not bad, but can you field?'

"The horse—he didn't tell me his name—makes this funny little whinny and trots on out to the outfield. I fungo a few out to him and he snags every one cleanly. The nag doesn't even need a mitt, he catches 'em between his teeth.

"I got to admit I'm pretty impressed by now. I've been to the track a lot in my time, and never has a horse performed for me like this one. I'm thinking, 'Maybe this is the left fielder I've been looking for . . .'

"So I say to him, 'You're pretty good, for a horse. But one more thing I gotta know. And it's important. Can you run?'

"'Run?' the horse says to me. 'If I could run, do you think I'd be out here looking for a job? I'd be at Belmont!'"

Dummy

Some baseball stories are so implausible they simply cannot be believed. Others are so implausible that you *want* to believe them even if they're not true. A story of the latter kind:

In the years before the turn of the century, there was a center fielder named Dummy Hoy. He wasn't very big, but he was fast. He stole bases and covered lots of ground in center, and some people think he belongs in the Hall of Fame.

Dummy got his nickname—his given name was William Ellsworth Hoy—from being a deaf-mute. Calling someone "Dummy" may seem cruel by contemporary standards, but it was in keeping with the rough-edged frontier habits of ballplayers back then. And you never heard a peep of complaint out of Dummy.

Dummy was an excellent lip-reader. Besides that, many of his teammates used sign language to communicate with him. He could talk, in a small, throaty squeak, but he mainly used his voice when playing the outfield. "When you played with him in the outfield, the thing was that you never called for a ball," recollected Tommy Leach, a former teammate. "You listened for him, and if he made this little squeaky sound, that meant he was going to take it." There never were any crack-ups in an outfield anchored by Dummy Hoy.

Dummy's biggest problem in baseball was when he hit. Unable to hear voices, he had to turn after every pitch to see what the ump had called. To help him out, umps began using hand signals—raising the right hand, for instance, so Dummy would know that the pitch was a strike.

Thus the practice spread around the league, and in time umpires routinely used hand signal to call balls and strikes for all players, not just deaf-mutes.

A Man Behind His Time

Managers of the past used to rely on another form of hand signal to call for relievers out in the bullpen. The signals, often very elaborate and extensive, became obsolete with the advent of the phone.

The last manager to use an antiquated system of hand signals was the antiquated Connie Mack, manager of the Philadelphia A's. According to Bob Considine, Mack had his pitching coach do a pantomime whenever the A's needed somebody from the pen. It was almost like playing charades. If the right-hander Joe Coleman was needed, the coach mimicked a man shoveling . . . coal. If he banged his fists against the fence at old Shibe Park in Philadelphia—the home of the A's—that meant to send in Carl Scheib. Get it?

The most complicated routine for the coach—Marcel Marceau should have applied for the job—required him to stoop in front of the dugout and act as if he were picking flowers. That—decoded—was the signal to bring in Dick

Fowler, who the always polite Connie Mack referred to as "Mr. Flowers."

Two Sketches: From the Thirties

1
WILD HOSS

Pepper Martin, wrote Glenn Dickey, played baseball "in the manner of the Allied troops storming Normandy in World War II." He blocked balls with his chest at third base, dove into the dirt, and did headfirst slides on the base paths well before Pete Rose was a twinkle in his parents' eyes.

Even from afar it's hard not to like a ballplayer of the type of Pepper Martin. You see his spiritual descendants around ball fields these days. He's Ryne Sandberg with a bloody nose, Bill Madlock with a country twang. Grantland Rice, the sportswriter, saw nothing great in any one of Martin's skills, but had to admit that overall he was indeed a "great ballplayer." He could beat you a lot of ways, but mostly he did it with speed and guile. He was, in the words of one baseball man, "a hard guy" who played on a team of hard guys, the St. Louis Gashouse Gang of the 1930s. Frank Frisch, Ducky Medwick, the Dean brothers, Pepper Martin—these were a bunch of rowdy, butt-kicking ballplayers who gave a nation, sunken under the weight of the Depression, something to cheer about.

A sportswriter dubbed Martin the "Wild Hoss of the Osage," referring to that part of Oklahoma where he was born and raised. His people were Tom Joad's people, hardscrabble folks whose farms turned to dust in the '30s and who knew the value of a dollar because of how much work it took to get one. In 1931 Martin's Cardinals met the Philadelphia A's of Lefty Grove and Jimmie Foxx, the two-time defending World Champions. The A's were a freight train of a ball team, packed with power and pitching. But if Pepper was impressed he did not act it.

Pepper did everything to the A's but undress them and

put them to bed at night. He hit, he stole bases, he scored runs. Kenesaw Mountain Landis, the commissioner of baseball who was taking in the Series, called Pepper over to his box to congratulate him on his fine play. "I wish I could change places with you," the Judge told Pepper. "Okay with me," said Pepper, faithful to his roots. "If you'll swap your fifty thousand dollars a year for my forty-five hundred."

Later in the Series, with Martin at bat and the game on the line, a concerned Connie Mack strode out to the mound to consult with his pitcher, George Earnshaw. The A's manager asked what Martin had been hitting.

"Everything we throw," Earnshaw said quietly.

2
MAN OF IRON

Lou Gehrig was to baseball what Gary Cooper was to the movies: a figure of unimpeachable integrity, massive and incorruptible, a hero. Cooper in fact played Gehrig in the film about the latter's life, *Pride of the Yankees*. Today both are seen as paradigms of manly virtue. Decent and God-fearing, yet strongly charismatic and powerful.

Though a titan in baseball annals, Gehrig off the field was about as much fun as oatmeal. Wholesome, respectable—and boring. Unlike his Yankee teammates Babe Ruth and Waite Hoyt, Lou did not drink strong spirits or curse or chase wild women late into the night. He sometimes brought his mother—"Mom Gehrig," as she was known to everyone—on road trips with the team. He was, said Rosy Ryan, "a grand fellow, but a little close. They used to claim he cut his own hair." Once Lou was asked on a live radio commercial how he grew up to be so big and strong. "By eating Wheaties," he said firmly. Trouble was, the sponsor of the spot was Huskies breakfast cereal, not Wheaties.

For much of his career Gehrig played in the huge, lurking shadow of Babe Ruth, who batted ahead of him in the ball-crunching Yankee lineup. The Babe was a great showman and terrific copy, and the modest, painfully shy first baseman suffered by contrast. (A modern parallel can be found in the Yankees of the late seventies when the loud-talking Reggie Jackson overshadowed the stolid and hardworking Thurman Munson in the media. Munson, coincidentally, died at a young age too.) As Ruth's powers declined and Gehrig came into his own as a power hitter in the early thirties, Lou's public relations problems diminished and he began to be appreciated for being the great, great ballplayer he was. His prominence has not lessened with time, either in the baseball record books or in our memories.

Ironically, as every schoolboy knows, this superhuman model of durability, this man of iron died, at age thirty-seven, of a debilitating neurological disorder now known as "Lou Gehrig's disease." Amyotrophic lateral sclerosis (ALS) attacks the muscles; in its later stages the victim is too weak to walk and needs a respirator to breathe. Complete immobility can occur. In 1925 Gehrig took over first base for the Yankees and did not let it go. Coolidge and Hoover came and went, FDR was elected—and Lou was on first base. Wall Street crashed, the Jazz Age ended and the Depression set in, the Reichstag burned, America embarked on a New Deal—and still, throughout it all, Gehrig was at his post, digging balls out of the dirt and rapping runners around, game after game after game. In 1939 he pulled himself out of the lineup and his consecutive-game streak ended after nearly fourteen complete seasons.

When that inevitable day came, when a new first baseman replaced the old, the players in the Yankee dugout were as quiet as at a funeral. Joe McCarthy was in that dugout, so was Joe DiMaggio. Gehrig sat at the end of the bench and stared blankly at the field, his face a mask. Lefty Gomez walked over to him and said, "Now you know how us pitchers feel when we've been knocked out of the box," but the joke didn't work. Gehrig didn't smile. He just sat there staring straight ahead at the field, and two years later he was dead.

The Catfish

One tough hombre—who wouldn't take any guff off Ty Cobb or John McGraw or any of the other hotheads of his time—was Bill Klem, the Old Arbitrator. Klem had one basic rule of arbitration: His side won. It was a simple rule, and it never failed him in forty years of umping.

The *Sporting News* called Klem "the No. 1 umpire of all time." He was an aged Solomon behind the plate, known for his absolute sureness, his rock-hard certainty. "I never thought eyesight was the most important thing in umpiring," he said. "The most important things are guts, honesty, common sense, a desire for fair play and an understanding of human nature." A few years ago ump Dale Ford was spotted wearing a T-shirt with the inscription, ONCE I THOUGHT I WAS WRONG, BUT I WAS MISTAKEN. This was a play on a famous saying of Klem's, who never missed a call in his heart. In the locker room after a game in 1941 he found himself thinking about a call he had made, questioning whether it was the right one. He submitted his resignation from baseball that day, and never umped another game in his life.

Klem had big lips and floppy ears, and when making a demonstrative call, "he'd let fly a rather fine spray from his mouth," according to New York Giants catcher Chief Meyers. For these traits—plus his angry sting—he earned the nickname "Catfish," though players only called him that to his face if they wanted to view the rest of the proceedings from the stands. The Catfish would brook nothing that could be interpreted as disrespect. "Son," he said to a rookie who disgustedly threw his bat in the air after a called third strike, "if that bat comes down, you're out of the game."

One of his confrontations with the fire-breathing manager of the Giants, John McGraw, is as famous as any in baseball. After a close call went against his team, McGraw shouted furiously, "I'm going all the way to the top, Klem.

And I'm going to get your job, so help me, if it's the last thing I ever do!"

The Old Arbitrator was as calm and controlled as his nemesis was hot.

"Mr. McGraw," he said matter of factly, "if it's possible for you to get my job, I don't want it."

His Father's Son

Mention the name of Bobo Newsom in baseball circles today and chances are you'll draw a laugh. Bobo, after all, was bandied about the major leagues like a call girl at a bachelor party, changing teams fifteen times in his long career. A record like that *is* kind of a joke.

But 1940 was no joke to Bobo. That was the year his dad died, the year he pitched for the Tigers in the World Series. Bobo won two games for Detroit over the Reds. He started and won the opener. In the fifth game, which came only days after his father's death, he crafted a masterpiece, a courageous three-hit shutout. Then, after only a day's rest he came back and pitched the seventh and final game, barely getting beat in a close, gritty thriller.

How did you do it? they asked. How did you pitch so well, Bobo?

Said Bobo, "My dad was lookin' down from a window in heaven tellin' me what to throw."

War Story

Baseball gave its all during the Second World War, no question. Joe DiMag, Teddy Ballgame, the Marine Corps' Bill Veeck (who lost a foot in action), Bob Feller, Warren Spahn and scores of others—they all pitched in, they all served, and they didn't come back till it was over over there.

It would not be quite correct, though, to say that baseball sentiment was unanimous in its support for the war effort.

There was the case, for instance, of the Tennessee minor league manager and his vanishing second basemen.

This manager, who shall remain anonymous, was holding his team at the top of the league standings when the U.S. Army drafted his best player, a second baseman. This was late in the season, and most observers thought the loss of a player of this caliber would cost the team the pennant.

Fortunately for the Trackers—a fictitious name—they had somebody in reserve who turned out to be even better than the man he replaced. He was sensational, an instant star whose great play must have brought him to the attention of his local Army recruiter. For he was gone from the team and in boot camp in less than a month.

One thing about the Trackers that year: they had depth. No sooner had Second Baseman No. 2 left than No. 3 stepped in, and *he* proved to be a veritable Joe Morgan, by far the best of the lot and possibly the best young prospect they'd ever seen in those parts. His draft notice came after a doubleheader in which he hit a grand slam and made an unassisted triple play.

"Jeezus Christ!" shouted the manager of the Trackers after being informed about the latest draftee. "You'd think they were going to fight this damned war around second base!"

Lefty and Joe

Lefty Gomez, the great Yankee left-hander and ballyard wit, tells this story about his old pal and teammate, Joe DiMaggio:

"Joe liked to play a shallow center field, you know. He was always telling me, 'I'll make 'em forget Speaker, I'll make 'em forget Speaker.' Tris Speaker, of course. The Cleveland Hall of Famer. Spoke used to play so shallow in center that he was practically a fifth infielder.

"Anyhow, one day I was pitching against Detroit, I think

it was. And somebody hit one a ton way out to center that Joe got his glove on but couldn't hold. Joe saved a lot more games for us than I could ever count, but this one got away from him. The ball went for a triple and some runs scored and we lost the game.

"So afterwards a bunch of us guys were sitting around at dinner. Me and Joe and some other people, talking about the game like we always did in those days. So here we were talking, and Joe goes into it again. 'I'll make 'em forget Speaker,' he's saying to us all, 'I'll make 'em forget Speaker.'

"I almost choked on my peas. 'Joe,' I said, 'if you don't move back in center a little, you'll make 'em forget Gomez!'"

In Your Face

The names of Joe DiMaggio and Ted Williams are inextricably linked in the baseball universe. They were rivals who played for rival cities whose deep civic pride is reflected in their intense devotion to their ball teams. They were the two best ballplayers of their generation, the generation that lost years to World War II, and both belong on any serious all-time American League all-star team.

Both were marvels to behold on a baseball diamond. DiMaggio, wrote Arnold Hano, "looked more like a great deer than a human, running lightly on his toes, head and neck stretched out, nostrils seemingly quivering, eyes searching for whatever he had to know." He was the classiest of center fielders, with an uncanny ability to anticipate where a batter was going to hit the ball and then *be* there, smoothly, easily, effortlessly.

Ted Williams, of the Red Sox, was the consummate hitter. He approached his time at bat with a perfectionist zeal: uncompromising, unflinching, totally absorbed in the act of making clean contact and driving the ball. He may not have become "the greatest hitter who ever lived," as he wished for himself when he was nineteen or twenty, but he came closer to it than any boy that age has a right to expect. Wrote Ed Linn, "For two decades he made the Red Sox exciting in the sheer anticipation of his next at bat."

After leaving the game DiMaggio turned down offers to manage and, true to his persona, has generally stayed aloof, occasionally accepting ceremonial roles with the Yankees or appearing at old-timer games. No less aware of the mystique surrounding him, and equally protective of his privacy, Ted Williams has taken a somewhat more active role in baseball since retiring. He was talked into taking a break from fishing the trout streams he loves to manage the Washington Senators (shifting to Texas) for a time in the late sixties and early seventies.

These days, if you're lucky, you can find him in the spring at Red Sox training camp in Winter Haven, Florida, where he dispenses tips on how to hit to young, would-be major leaguers. Now in his late sixties, he putts about the practice diamonds in a golf cart, looking larger and fuller than the skinny, gangly-boned kid that inspired the nickname "The Splendid Splinter." But the young hopefuls still listen attentively, as well they should. "Ted Williams on hitting," remarked Ira Berkow, "is Lindbergh on flying, Picasso on painting, and Little Richard on the Tutti-Frutti."

But we should not let this benign picture of an aging and patriarchal Ted Williams deceive us. The man was as arrogant a ballplayer as ever lived. Though California-born, he was anything but mellow. He was defiant, insolent and supremely proud. His career-long battle with the press makes Dave Kingman look like a master of public relations. If, as has been said, the Red Sox and their fans are family, and Fenway Park their home, then Williams was the genius son whose at times indefensible behavior outraged nearly everyone, including his supporters. A group in the left field stands at Fenway heckled him like he was a New York Yankee, and in a couple of inglorious episodes he actually spat

on some of the more outspoken paying customers, who may
have deserved it. The nastiness of the feud embittered the
entire Boston family, most of all Williams. And he never
gave in. *Never.*

In his last at bat in his last game ever at Fenway or
anywhere else, Williams hit a home run. *A home run!* The
people in the seats couldn't believe their eyes. They jumped
to their feet and yelled, begging Williams to tip his cap, to
wave, to acknowledge in some way their cheers. It was a
plea for reconciliation, and Williams turned them down flat.
Did not tip his cap as he rounded the bases, did not come out
of the dugout to wave to the fans. As John Updike wrote,
"Gods do not answer letters."

Mickey Mantle said Williams was the greatest hitter he
ever saw. "He lived for his next turn at bat," Eddie Collins,
another sweet swinger, said in awe. Williams had great vision and gunfighter reflexes to go along with another important quality for a hitter: self-discipline. "I never saw him
swing at a bad ball," umpire George Pipgras said. "He'd
take a ball an inch or two off the plate and never flinch. I'll
tell you, he kept you on your toes, the way he took pitches.
And when he took a pitch and you called it a strike, you
couldn't help but think you'd missed it."

What Williams knew cannot be taught. Yet he was the
model craftsman, with the arrogance to think that he could
perfect the mechanics of the batting motion. He would not
bend to the defensive maneuver employed by teams around
the league in which they put three infielders on the right side
of the diamond when he hit. He kept swinging the way he
always did—partly out of his professed desire to help the
Red Sox with home runs rather than cheap singles through
the left side, but also because he could not bear to let outside
factors affect the purity of his stroke.

One story about Williams may sum up his personality.
One time Virgil "Fire" Trucks struck him out to end a game,
and then afterward took the ball over to the Red Sox clubhouse to get Williams to sign it. Ted went along with the

request, not saying any more than was necessary. A week or so later he got another chance to face Trucks, and this time hit one of his pitches over the roof at Tiger Stadium.

As Williams went into his home run trot, he called out to Trucks, "Go get that one and I'll autograph it for you too."

In your face, buddy.

The Larsen Game

Of all the pitchers to compete in the World Series, only one has achieved perfection: Don Larsen. His feat is unsurpassable.

Bill Bevens came very, very close to throwing a no-hitter in a Series game. But twenty-seven up, twenty-seven down? Only Larsen can claim it. "I'm not what you call a real praying man," he has said, "but once I was out there, in the eighth or ninth, I said to myself, 'Help me out, somebody.'" It's highly unlikely that that Somebody will ever again help a pitcher mow down every hitter in the ultimate baseball event. For one golden afternoon in 1956, Don Larsen, an otherwise mediocre pitcher, lived in a state of grace.

Another reason why Larsen's feat may never be duplicated has to do with the circumstances of the game itself. That World Series between the Yankees and Dodgers was an extraordinary confluence of men and events. Never again will we see those men on a field together playing a game of such importance on a day like that. The game was utterly unique, unlike any other played before or since.

This may seem the most banal of observations, but not when you remember that controversial last call. Would Don Larsen have risen to heavenly heights without the earthly help of Babe Pinelli?

To the game:

Top of the ninth, two out. Twenty-six Dodgers had come up, twenty-six had gone down. The Yankees were ahead in the game, but the score seemed almost incidental to the gut-grabbing drama between hitter and pitcher. In the '47 Series another Yankee pitcher, Bill Bevens, had taken a no-hitter into the ninth inning and lost it with two men out. It could happen again.

Pinch-hitting for the Dodgers was Dale Mitchell, a late-season acquisition. He represented Brooklyn's last chance, and he let it pass by him. With a count of one ball and two strikes, Mitchell watched the third strike disappear in the catcher's mitt. That was it, perfection was sealed, and Yogi Berra, the catcher, rushed out to be the first of the Yankees to embrace their pitcher.

Leave it to Yogi to turn high drama into comedy. He was so excited he jumped straight into Don Larsen's arms, whose first words after gaining baseball immortality were, "Damn Yogi, you're heavy."

As the Yankees celebrated, Dale Mitchell's emotions turned from frustration to anger. Like Ralph Branca or Tracy Stallard, Mitchell belongs to that select, if hard-luck, group of victims that accompany every heroic baseball act. But he has never accepted this role gladly, maintaining even today that home plate ump Babe Pinelli blew that last call. "Everybody ran off the field so fast, there was no chance to argue," he told Hal Bock a couple years ago. "The pitch was away. It wasn't a strike." Mitchell added scornfully, "Pinelli retired after that Series. He should have retired before it."

Babe Pinelli, the other major figure in this historic tableau, did call it quits after The Larsen Game, perhaps with the understanding that for an umpire there could be no finer way to go out. In baseball terms, he had been to the mountaintop and seen all there was to see. After Larsen's performance nothing else would do, even the greatest of pitchers would seem second-rate.

After Pinelli died, at age eighty-nine in a convalescent home near San Francisco, an unlikely defender of his controversial third-strike call arose in the person of Dr. Stephen Jay Gould, a Harvard professor and a respected science author. Gould, a devout Yankees fan, argued in *The New York*

Times that even if that last pitch *was* outside, Pinelli was right in making the call he did. Dale Mitchell, claimed Gould, "may not take a close pitch with so much on the line. Context matters. Truth is a circumstance, not a spot."

Gould concluded, "By long and recognized custom, by any concept of Justice, Dale Mitchell had to swing at anything close. It was a strike—a strike low and outside. Babe Pinelli, umpiring his last game, ended with his finest, most perceptive, his most truthful moment.

"Babe Pinelli, arbiter of history, walked into the locker room and cried."

Lights Out

Baseball needs men like the legendary Bill Veeck. He never played in the major leagues but in his own way he contributed as much to the game as anybody.

He signed the first black, Larry Doby, to play in the American League. His St. Louis Browns featured for one at bat the only midget to ever make the big leagues, Eddie Gaedel. It was Veeck's idea to put ivy on the walls at Wrigley Field.

He was a baseball owner who did not need a gaggle of MBA's around him to come to a decision. Throughout his life he has drunk like a sailor and smoked packs of cigarettes a day. A war injury gave him an artificial leg. "Sometimes when seated," Roy Blount observed, "Veeck will suddenly press the button that operates the knee joint of his peg leg: Snap, there it is, as if from nowhere, a peg leg sticking straight out in front of him." Then Veeck will tap cigarette ashes into the hole at the knee joint.

A hustler and a P. T. Barnum–style promoter, Veeck's most outrageous stunt was in Milwaukee, where he installed an outfield fence that could be moved in or out depending on what best served his team. His team, goes the story, was in a jam late in a home game against its most hated rival. The bases were loaded, no one was out, and up at the plate was the opposing team's cleanup hitter, who had already smacked a home run and a double in the game.

Suddenly, the lights went out.

In the ensuing confusion, both teams had to leave the field and play had to be stopped. Bill Veeck explained it as "an act of God."

Nobody ever found out who exactly turned off the lights, but the enraged commissioner of baseball called Veeck into his office and declared that henceforth, in our national pastime, "There shall be no more acts of God."

Reprise:
Casey and the Sparrow

Everybody must know about the time a sparrow flew out from under Casey Stengel's cap. But not so well-known is the time the Dodgers tried to repeat the trick years later.

The first time, in 1918, was magical. When a sparrow crashed against the bullpen wall at old Ebbets Field in Brooklyn, the genius of inspiration alighted on Stengel, who was standing nearby. He cradled the stunned bird in his hands and returned to the dugout. An inning later, with all the crowd watching him, Stengel bent over and doffed his cap, from which flew the now-alert sparrow. The fans at Ebbets were no more amazed by what they saw than the early cavemen had been at the invention of fire.

Nearly a half century later an old and bent Casey Stengel, who should have known better, was prevailed upon to try his famous trick again at an old-timer's game in Dodger Stadium. Some public relations people rounded up a sparrow from a Los Angeles pet shop. To get the bird quieted down, somebody had the bright idea of spinning it rapidly around by its tail. Casey obligingly did his part, but after he doffed his cap the bird fell to the ground like a rock. It wasn't dead, only dozing.

The moral: You cannot rubber-stamp genius. The muses

will not be bullied; they come and go as they like, regardless of the opinions of public relations people.

In the Land of Make-Believe

Once upon a time there was a ballplayer who made the impossible look routine. He was named Willie Howard Mays. When Willie was born the attending physician remarked on the unusually large size of the infant's hands. From the very start, Willie was one of the chosen ones.

To talk of Mays is to talk in superlatives. "Willie Mays was a force of nature who overcame other forces of nature," Larry Merchant wrote. Reggie Jackson said, "You used to think if the score was 5–0, he'd hit a five-run homer." He was the most gifted player of his generation, and probably the best all-around in the second half of the twentieth century. And it's difficult to imagine how the next century could come up with a better center fielder. Certainly none of the present-day contenders—not Dawson, not Murphy, not Henderson—can do it all like he did it all, game in and game out, every day he stepped across the lines. Bill Rigney, the ex–Giants manager who's now an A's executive, recalls watching a splendid game by Rickey Henderson when he was with Oakland. "Rickey, that's the best game I ever saw you play," Rigney told him, adding: "But that's the way No. 24 played *every* day."

So what made Willie Mays so great, such a joy to watch? "All in all, I most enjoy watching him run the bases," Roger Angell wrote. "He cuts the base like a racing car, looking back over his shoulder at the ball, and lopes grandly into third, and everyone who has watched him finds himself laughing with excitement and shared delight." Running the bases, his Giants cap flying off behind him, making a basket catch in the outfield, throwing runners out from deep center, climbing the fence to make a catch—in these ways, and a hundred more, Mays was, as Roger Kahn said, "the ultimate combination of the professional full of talent and the amateur, a word that traces to the Latin *amator,* or lover, and suggests one who brings passion to what he does." One observer likened him to Rousseau's Natural Man. The veteran sportswriter Frank Graham said simply, "There's just no such thing as getting used to the guy."

Willie's first manager in the big leagues was Leo Durocher. Early in the 1951 season, with Mays still in the minors, Leo called to tell him he was bringing him up to the Giants. Mays was excited, but reluctant about making the move.

"I can't hit the pitching up there," he said nervously.

"What are you hitting in Minneapolis?" Durocher asked.

"Uh, four seventy-seven I think," came the weak reply.

"Four seventy-seven?" said Durocher, astonished. "Do you think you can hit two-fucking-seventy for me?"

Over time Mays of course hit considerably better than that, as Leo will be the first to tell you. For him—and many others, to be sure—Mays is *It*—the standard against which all modern ballplayers are to be measured.

Mays made a catch thirty years ago in a World Series that was so marvelous it's known today simply as The Catch. Arnold Hano, who was sitting in the stands that day, wrote an entire book centered on that one incident. Not as prolific, but no less eloquent, was Harvey Kuenn who, after seeing Mays make an over-the-head catch of a line drive, said, "I didn't know whether to laugh, shit or go blind."

It should also be remembered that once Mays caught a ball he knew what to do with it. Baserunners ran on him at their peril. After a Mays missile from deep center nabbed a runner at home plate tagging from third, eyewitness Whitey Lockman said, "It wasn't a throw, it was a *pitch.*"

Another thing to keep in mind about Willie is that for the bulk of his career he hit and ran and caught and threw in the Sing Sing of baseball stadiums, Candlestick Park. Enough has already been said about that windswept mausoleum of a stadium, and it is devoutly to be hoped that the Good Fathers and Mothers of San Francisco find it in their hearts to blow it to smithereens. But it remains a part of the Mays legacy that he was able to thrive in surroundings that humbled so many other players. Roberto Clemente said, "You had to be out of your mind to play the outfield in that park. How do you catch a ball in that wind—unless you're Willie Mays?"

But there's no need to belabor the point. If you saw him play, you know. Nothing more really needs to be said. It's not a bunch of sentimental blooey cooked up by misty-eyed old-timers. The guy was *that* good.

But not at the end. In his last years he was not the Willie Mays you remembered, he was just another washed-up old ballplayer who didn't know when to get out. Stumbling and falling on the base paths, swinging weakly at third strikes, letting fly balls drop in center that in his youth he would have snagged in his back pocket. Age has reduced many a great name—Spahn, Aaron, Ernie Banks—but somehow you never expected it to happen to Willie Mays. "Growing old," he admitted before he retired, "is just a helpless hurt."

If they ever make a movie about Willie's life, they won't end it on this sad human note, however. Hollywood will instead choose a more upbeat finale, one that will let audiences go home smiling. In this celluloid version of reality, an old and tired Willie Mays will be traded at the very end of his career to New York, where he started in the majors. San Francisco never appreciated him anyway, so it will seem especially appropriate to the scriptwriters that he return to the city that loved him always.

Jump cut to Willie's first game as a Met. Not coincidentally—these Hollywood filmmakers are crafty types—the game is against his old team, the Giants. Willie felt jilted being traded by the Giants, so he would like nothing better than to beat them with a home run, a single heroic swat that would cut through the bittersweet passage of time and make everything right again, if only for an instant.

Amazingly, Willie does it. He hits that home run to beat the Giants. As the crowd erupts the camera turns to Pete

Hamill (playing himself), who says in a tremulous voice, "The ball flew high and proud through the New York air, over the infielders, traveling sweetly and purely, obliterating the rain, landing at last in some summer afternoon in 1957. Willie Mays ran the bases, carrying all those summers on his forty-one-year-old shoulders, jogging in silence, while people in the stands pumped their arms at the skies and hugged each other and even, here and there, cried. It was a glittering moment of repair, in a city that has been starved too long for joy. Don't tell me New York isn't going to make it. Willie Mays is home."

And that's the way the movie would end. With Willie Mays home again, with Willie Mays defeating time.

Aw, but who would believe it? It'd just be another silly Hollywood fantasy. Real life isn't like that.

Famous Last Gasps

Old ballplayers may not know how to retire gracefully, but they do know how to die.

Connie Mack played in the nineteenth century and managed the Philadelphia A's into the second half of the twentieth. Asked if he'd ever quit baseball, he said, "If I did, I'd die in two weeks." The ancient patrician did die, in 1956, a relatively short time after his beloved Athletics left Philadelphia for Kansas City.

When Tiny Bonham, a pitcher, was on his deathbed, he told a visitor, "They're hitting me all over the field and I can't get them out." We all should have such good closing lines.

But one James Whyte Davis may have had the best last word of all. As is noted in *The Fireside Book of Baseball,* Davis asked to be buried in his baseball suit and that the flag of the New York Knickerbockers, for whom he played in the

1850s, be wrapped around him in his coffin. Further, he
wanted his headstone to read:

3
Public Men, Private Lives

"Too many people think an athlete's life can be an open book. . . . The newspapermen come around and want to know about your private life. They say the public wants to know. Hell, I think just they want to know. You might get a hundred thousand people out to see a game someday, but you wouldn't get fifteen to come hear what I did last night."

—BOB GIBSON, Hall of Fame pitcher

Mister Cobb

IF, BY INVERSION, 1974 was Babe Ruth's year—the year Henry Aaron broke Ruth's career homer mark—then 1985, when Pete Rose surpassed the all-time hit record, could be considered Ty Cobb's. There could not be a story about Rose without some mention of the man whose record he was chasing. Rose above all was aware of the connection, having named his young son Tyler. And for good luck the Reds carried a bust of Cobb with them on road trips throughout the year.

Like the man who broke his record, Tyrus Raymond Cobb was a ferocious competitor. His father, who was shot dead by his mother in a bizarre accident in Cobb's rookie season, told his son, "Don't come home a failure." And he most assuredly did not. Cobb came at you, spikes flying, and he kept coming at you until you quit or were beaten. He was a man with the instincts of an alley fighter and the ballplaying gifts of a god. No less an authority on toughness than General Douglas MacArthur wrote the foreword to his autobiography. Cobb fought you with his bat and spikes and, if those weren't enough, he fought you with his fists. One season he jumped in the stands and beat a heckler unconscious, receiving a suspension and a fine. Nobody messed with Ty Cobb.

Stan Musial said that if Cobb were alive today he'd hit .350 a year. Anyone who has charted his mind-boggling statistics—John Updike called him "the Einstein of average"—would probably agree. Cobb possessed superior, whiplike quickness with his bat combined with a daring, hell-on-wheels baserunning style. Before a series against the Tigers, Red Sox catcher Lou Criger was quoted as saying, "This Cobb is one of those ginks with a lot of flash, but he doesn't fool me. Watch him wilt when it gets tough. I'll cut him down to size." Cobb made Criger eat his words on his first time at bat the next day. Hitting a curveball through the infield for a single, Cobb shouted to Criger behind the plate that he would be running on every pitch. And he did. On the first pitch, he stole second. On the second pitch, he stole third. Then, dancing down the line, taunting the pitcher and an utterly chagrined Lou Criger, he yelled, "Here I come!" and stole home on the next pitch. Baseball, the way Cobb played it.

But if you kept up with all the Rose-Cobb media hype or, for that matter, are already familiar with Cobb's history in baseball, anecdotes like these may not come as much of a surprise. Of more compelling interest is what Cobb did after he quit playing ball. Perhaps because we want our heroes to be giant-sized and eternally young, most of the recent stories about Cobb have centered on his career as a player—not the painful and sad years that were to follow.

Ty Cobb left the game for good in 1928, after more than two decades of playing and managing. He was then forty-one. When he got out he was determined to show that, unlike so many other ex-stars, he had the skill and business savvy to succeed off the field too. He achieved that success, but not without cost.

Cobb was elected to the Hall of Fame ahead of Babe Ruth, but only three people in all of professional baseball attended his funeral in 1961. According to Al Stump, who cowrote Cobb's autobiography, he earned millions from investments in Coca-Cola stock and real estate. But the rewards, and the respect he gained from his peers, were of the bitterest sort at the end. Toward the end of his life, ravaged by cancer, he became a Howard Hughesian figure with a head full of paranoias. He trusted no one, booby-trapping his California mansion and assaulting an ex-wife. He took

Librium to control his violent temper and convulsive mood swings. For months his eighteen-room mansion was lit only by candlelight and had no running water. Cobb, a millionaire, would not pay a sixteen-dollar electric bill until his lawsuit against the utilities company was settled.

He was a terror to himself and to others. He lost all his friends from baseball; they would not tolerate his outbursts over what seemed trivialities.Though there is record of his philanthropy, Cobb repeatedly practiced the one thing that the playwright Tennessee Williams called unforgivable: deliberate cruelty toward other human beings. Al Stump saw him throw a salt shaker at a waitress who was serving them. And when Cobb got fan mail requesting his autograph, he burned the letters and used the stamps enclosed by the autograph seekers for his own correspondence. For an ex-ballplayer, there can be no more cynical act than that. Mocking the child in himself, the child that could not come home a failure.

Love Story:
Marilyn and Joe

The ballplayer and the movie star met in the spring of 1952, the year after the ballplayer had retired from one of the greatest careers in the history of the game. The ballplayer's name was Joe DiMaggio. The movie star was Marilyn Monroe. Their bittersweet love story remains one of the most fascinating American romances of this century, for it brings together two larger-than-life figures from two of this country's most favorite obsessions, baseball and the movies. Since Marilyn is dead and Joe, to his credit, has staunchly refused to talk about her or their time together, what we know of their courtship and short, tumultuous marriage comes from secondhand sources—friends of the pair, close observers and acquaintances and, of course, sheer gossip. Ah, but such delightful and absorbing gossip it is!

In his biography of DiMaggio, Gene Schoor tells how the slugger and his future wife met.

After the 1951 season Joe retired from the game, turning down a hundred-thousand-dollar contract—in those days, very big money—because his tremendous pride in himself would not let him appear on a ball field at less than his best. "I haven't got that feeling that I used to have—that I can walk up there and hit any pitcher who ever lived," he said. Quitting relieved him of enormous responsibility, and in the spring of the following year he felt as good as he had in a long, long time. Freed of the pressures of training camp, there were no great demands on him or his time. The monkey was off his back.

That spring Gus Zernial, a muscular young Philadelphia A's outfielder, was coming off a big year with the bat. Some were calling him "the next DiMaggio." Zernial had a good physique and a colorful nickname—"Ozark Ike"—which helped make him an attractive personality. In the fifties the big Hollywood studios found they could get good publicity by posing one of their starlets with a major league ball-player. The photos were invariably corny, but newspapers around the country ate them up. So Ozark Ike was recruited to pose with a fast-rising actress named Marilyn Monroe, whose latest movie, *Clash by Night,* was set to be released in June.

Marilyn held a bat in her hands and went into a crouch. Ozark Ike, supposedly instructing her on the fine art of hitting, draped his arms around her body and wore a smile like he was the luckiest guy in the world.

When the picture ran in the papers it caught the eye of at least one interested party. At an exhibition game Joe Di-Maggio cornered Zernial to ask him about the beautiful blonde in the photograph. Zernial told him the name of the Hollywood agent who was handling Marilyn and who had set up the session.

"Thanks," said DiMaggio, who soon called the agent to ask him a favor. He wanted a date with one of his clients.

At the time of her first date with the most famous baseball player in the world, Marilyn Monroe was twenty-six. She had been in Hollywood for some time, and she was fast becoming somebody. Champagne had become her favorite drink. Successfully making the move from being a bit player to the name above the title, she had a number of films in release and, to the surprise of her studio, Twentieth Century-Fox, had received largely good reviews. The *New York Daily News* called her "the new blonde bombshell of Hollywood." After her performance in *Monkey Business* one critic wrote, "She disproves more than adequately the efficacy of the old stage rule about not turning one's back to the audience." The reviews of this time naturally focus not on her skills as an actress, which were still developing, but on her physical attributes, which had already developed quite nicely. Norman Mailer said at this stage of her life she looked as if she were "fed on sexual candy." When she appeared at a formal banquet in Los Angeles, the majority of men, dressed in tuxes and accompanied by their wives, whistled and stamped their feet as she walked in.

Their date was set for seven, at a Hollywood restaurant. Marilyn arrived at nine. Joe stood up and greeted her politely, not showing any irritation over being made to wait so long.

They didn't say much over dinner. Joe knew about as much about the movie business as Marilyn did about baseball, which was nothing. But Marilyn has written that she was impressed by the way DiMaggio carried himself, his athletic bearing and his tasteful, conservative dress. He was not what she expected, not slick and overbearing. His black hair even had a distinguished touch of gray in it.

One account of their romance claims that Marilyn pretended not to know who Joe DiMaggio was when told he wanted to go out with her. True or not, she had a convincing demonstration of his fame over dinner. Mickey Rooney, a big star in Hollywood at the time, came up to their table and acted deferential around Joe, regaling them with stories about some of the great things he had done on the Yankees and what a treat it had been to watch him play.

Afterward Joe offered to see Marilyn home in a cab, but she had brought her own car. She then asked Joe if he needed a lift back to his hotel. He said yes.

Few words were spoken on the drive to the hotel, just as at dinner. But communication of another sort must have been going on. When they reached the hotel Joe said he wasn't that sleepy. Would Marilyn mind if they drove around a while longer?

Something happened. "My heart jumped," Marilyn would say later. "All of a sudden I was full of happiness to be with Joe."

Probably only one man alive could have been that self-composed with Marilyn Monroe on a first date, and that man was Joe DiMaggio. As a ballplayer and after, he has been a model of self-possession. "Only Joe Louis matched DiMaggio for pure athlete's dignity," wrote Jimmy Cannon. Gay Talese, noting DiMaggio's "sad and haunted" expression, likened him to a matador. If he went hitless in a game he brooded alone in magisterial silence; he felt he was letting his teammates down and that feeling tore him up inside. "Everybody knew Joe DiMaggio and could depend on him and there was never any trouble when Joe DiMaggio played center field," Jimmy Breslin wrote. "Our wars had enemies to hate and heroes to glorify, and the summers were soft and the music was slow."

Everybody knew what Joe DiMaggio meant, and that included Joe DiMaggio. His father emigrated from Sicily, where his family had been fishermen for generations, and found a home in San Francisco. When the young DiMaggio returned to San Francisco after his triumphant rookie season with the Yankees, the Italian immigrant fishermen who docked their boats at Fisherman's Wharf carried him around the streets on their shoulders.

In 1941, with Europe at war, a song about Joltin' Joe DiMaggio and his famous hitting streak made it to the popular record charts. A quarter of a century later Paul Simon paid homage to him in the hit song "Mrs. Robinson." Simon, a Yankee fan when growing up, tried to explain the reasons for DiMaggio's lingering appeal: "It has something to do with heroes. People who are all good and no bad in them at all. That's the way I always saw Joe DiMaggio."

Perfection is a terrible burden for a human being to carry, and the way DiMaggio chose to do it was through dignified restraint. He never showed emotion on a ball field. One of the most famous catches in World Series history—Brooklyn left fielder Al Gionfriddo's remarkable running stab in the '47 Series off a ball hit by DiMaggio—is remembered as much for the catch as the fact that the stoical Yankee showed his temper on the play, kicking the dirt on the base paths after realizing he was out. DiMaggio's reserve on the field carried over into his private life. Wary of outsiders, he was aloof even among his teammates and close friends. An entry in Marilyn Monroe's diary, recounting her first impressions of Joe, describe him as being as "shy as I was. No jokes that I can remember. Not then. Not even any compliments."

But women have a way of breaking down even the most fiercely guarded male defenses, and that is apparently what happened to Joe. He fell for Marilyn, hard. After being let off at the hotel that first night, Joe could not wait to call her. He sat around his suite as long as he could, then dialed Marilyn's number. It was after midnight.

By this time Marilyn had gone to bed. Her busy shooting schedule precluded much of a social life, and she was tired. She had an early call on the set in the morning and needed the rest. The phone jangled her awake.

It was Joe. Asking for a date. Tomorrow evening sound good?

No. I'm busy.

Well what about the next night?

Sorry. You're sweet, but no.

By Gene Schoor's account, Joe tried again the next day and got the same answer. He called her again and again over the next few days, trying to get her to go out with him. "Everything was at stake for him, all the time," an admirer said about the way Joe DiMaggio conducted himself on a ball field. And it may have been true for him in real life too, after he met Marilyn Monroe. Everything suddenly was at stake for him. He had to see her.

But Marilyn refused, saying this was a bad time for her. She really didn't want to get involved with anybody.

After Joe called and called and Marilyn turned him down every time, he finally gave up. Quit phoning her. Quit trying to get her to change her mind.

A week or so passed. Then Joe got a call himself. It was from Marilyn. She had been thinking it over. Maybe dinner together did sound pretty good, after all.

Joe and Marilyn's relationship, in the words of Monroe biographer Fred Lawrence Guiles, was probably doomed from the start. The two, he says, had very little in common besides a healthy sexual appetite. Marilyn was young and on the upswing in her career while Joe was nearing forty, done with baseball and weary of always being center stage.

Though both loners at heart, they weren't very good in private. Marilyn read books and Joe did not. Marilyn admired intellectuals (exchanging signed photographs with Albert Einstein and later marrying the playwright Arthur Miller) and Joe scorned them. Marilyn loved to dance, Joe had two left feet. Joe cared little for the movie business except as to how it affected Marilyn, and Marilyn showed a similar disinterest in baseball. The couple primarily enjoyed fishing on Joe's yacht, *The Yankee Clipper,* and making love. Marilyn called her bedmate "my slugger."

The two quarreled frequently. The arguments generally centered on Marilyn's movie career. Joe did not like the Hollywood scene and wanted Marilyn to get out. He especially did not like the tramp roles she was given—in *Niagara* she played an adulteress whose dress, noted a critic, "is cut so low you can see her knees"—feeling that Hollywood was exploiting her looks and her innocent nature. Considerable tension existed between DiMaggio and some of Marilyn's oldest movie friends, who disparaged him as a big lunk trying to wreck a promising career.

Joe's temper, seldom seen by baseball fans, got an airing around Marilyn. During the shooting of *Gentlemen Prefer Blondes,* they engaged in a wall-rattling shouting match in her dressing room. He became her protector. He asked her to conceal her breasts more in public, and when around him she did dress more discreetly. Almost as soon as they started going out Joe began trying to persuade Marilyn to leave Hollywood behind and come up to live with him in his home in San Francisco. Joe either would not or could not understand how much his lover's career meant to her and how deeply held was her aspiration to become a good actress.

Marilyn went back and forth on whether or not to marry Joe. Sometimes she thought, He's the one; other times she knew it was impossible. In her heart she must have known she was never cut out to be a San Francisco housewife. No man, not even the great Joe DiMaggio (nor Arthur Miller), could complete her.

Still, he *was* intriguing, she had to admit that. Movie stars and other famous people looked up to him, seemed awed by him. He had his own undeniable charisma and a smoldering, mysterious charm.

Indeed, DiMaggio's charisma may have been another source of friction for the couple. Marilyn, the reigning sex goddess of American cinema, was used to being the center of attention wherever she went. At a party or a restaurant, people made a fuss over her, men especially. But with Di-Maggio on her arm, things were different. Men sought *him* out—to shake his hand, get an autograph, bestow a compliment—leaving Marilyn, all buttoned up in a high-collared dress, on the outside.

On January 14, 1954, baseball's Yankee Clipper and the former Norma Jean Mortensen were married in a private ceremony in San Francisco Municipal Court. The bride looked ravishing in a nut-brown suit with white ermine collar, while the groom wore a tasteful blue suit. This was the second marriage for both. In what could be interpreted as a symbol of the power struggle that persisted throughout their relationship and eventually split them apart, a few close friends of DiMaggio's from San Francisco attended, while nobody from Hollywood was there. It's said that Marilyn only decided to marry Joe two days before, and had put in a call to Twentieth Century-Fox that morning to inform the studio of her plans for the day.

As the newlyweds emerged from the judge's chambers, packs of headline-hungry reporters and flash photographers set upon them. This was nothing new. From their first date, press interest in the couple ran high. Liz and Dick had nothing on them. Photos of the two were splashed across every newspaper and two-bit scandal sheet in the country. Curiosity about them was immense and grew accordingly as rumors of their impending marriage spread.

Later in their marriage, on a trip to Japan, mobs of adoring fans met them at the stopover at the Honolulu airport. When they arrived in Tokyo, more screaming fans crowded in to see them. They were loved beyond exasperation.

The scene at the San Francisco courthouse was no different. Marilyn and Joe, smiling grimly, fought through the crowd to Joe's dark blue Cadillac. Their destination was a southern California mountain resort outside Palm Springs. They wanted to get away from the crush of people, the reporters, the prying questions.

Not able to make Palm Springs that day, they stopped for the night in Paso Robles, a forlorn little desert town in inland California, and found a motel that looked clean and neat. The proprietor of the motel, a man named Ernie Sharpe, was reportedly relaxing in front of the TV when a customer walked in the front door of his office.

"Hi," said Joe DiMaggio. "We'd like a room with a television set."

*   *   *

Things began to go awry almost from the beginning.

Marilyn moved into Joe's house in the Marina district of San Francisco, acquiescing for a time to her husband's most fervent wish for her. But she found she did not really fit into his world. DiMaggio *was* San Francisco in a way she was becoming Hollywood. He walked along the streets of North Beach like a good and benevolent ruler. Supposedly he never had to pay for a drink in the city; his many friends and admirers would not allow it.

There were other problems as well. A hard man to get to know, Joe was sullen and uncommunicative at times, telling his new bride to leave him alone. In his strong Italian-American heritage, the woman, though an important and influential figure, had a prescribed role in the household, one that Marilyn was not cut out to play. Joe, too, had a tight group of friends who were loyal as brothers to him. As Joe protected Marilyn, they protected him.

One night Marilyn was seen running from Joe on the San Francisco docks, crying hysterically. What the pair did may have been news around the world, but among the tightly knit Italian immigrant families who lived along the wharf, the DiMaggios' marital spats were nobody's business but their own.

By April their marriage was already tearing at the edges. For a change of scenery they decided to take an extended honeymoon to Japan. While there, Marilyn was asked to go to Korea to entertain American combat troops, and she jumped at the chance. Joe, whose business commitments prevented him from going with her, reluctantly gave his okay.

Marilyn's short side trip to Korea had a lasting impact on her. She was contributing to the war effort, and the boys loved her. She felt needed and wanted by them. She sang and danced and the U.S. combat troops, hundreds of thousands of them, roared their approval at her performances.

Returning to Japan to be with her husband, Marilyn was wide-eyed as a child. "It was so wonderful, Joe," she said excitedly to him. "You've never heard such cheering."

"Yes," Joe told her. "I have."

Their breakup came later in the year, at the filming of *The Seven Year Itch,* the marvelous Billy Wilder comedy. With Wilder directing, Marilyn was shooting a scene on the streets of Manhattan in which a passing subway train sends a stream of air up through a grate and blows her white pleated skirt up around her thighs. There may be no more famous moment in all of screen history, but one man watching did not approve.

DiMaggio, who had accompanied his wife to New York to be on the set of her new movie, was furious. The scene had to be shot and reshot until it was perfect, and with each new take the crowd of people on the street called for more and more of Marilyn's body to be exposed. It was insulting and humiliating for Joe, who left quietly. But that night, alone with his wife in their suite at the St. Regis, angry shouts erupted. They were so loud that other guests in the hotel complained downstairs. The next morning Joe checked out of the St. Regis, and their marriage was over in everything but name.

The announcement of their separation, nine months after being married, hit the papers like D Day. Flocks of reporters descended upon Marilyn's Laurel Canyon house, where Joe stayed part of the time. He had packed his things up and was going. Few tears were shed by movie people, many of whom felt vindicated. Joe was bad news, a bad influence on Marilyn. Now Joe was out of the picture and Marilyn was staying. Bye-bye, slugger.

Distraught and in tears, Marilyn stayed out of view inside the house. As Joe left someone asked him where he was going.

"Back to San Francisco," he said. "That's my home."

After their divorce came a brief bit of burlesque. Joe was a jealous lover—and not apparently without cause. Roy Blount, Jr., the writer, recounts an escapade by DiMaggio and Frank Sinatra that's straight out of a Doris Day–Rock Hudson bedroom farce.

A few days after the divorce became final, DiMaggio and Sinatra reportedly set out with some pals to see if they could catch Marilyn in bed with another man. It was late at night, and they parked well away from where they thought Marilyn's tryst was taking place. The singer testified in court that he stayed behind at the car, while DiMaggio and cohorts snuck up to the house. In a rush they broke down the door and turned flashlights onto a woman's face.

But it was not Marilyn. They had busted into the wrong place. Later the aggrieved woman settled out of court for seventy-five hundred dollars.

Marilyn Monroe remains a very sensitive subject with Joe DiMaggio, now in his seventies. He does not discuss her with reporters. Some time ago Roger Kahn asked him for his cooperation on a biography Kahn was writing about him. DiMaggio said he'd answer anything Kahn asked him, as long as there were no questions about Marilyn.

DiMaggio's close friends are equally circumspect. They will not speak on the record about Marilyn and Joe, lest they incur Joe's disfavor. The best man at their wedding, a San Francisco restaurateur, hung up on this writer when questioned on a matter concerning the couple.

No doubt DiMaggio avoids talking about Marilyn, at least in part, because it brings him pain. There are those who believe Joe may have had a terrible divination of Marilyn's fate, and in his efforts to bring her to San Francisco sought to divert her from it. "DiMaggio," writes Fred Guiles in his biography of Monroe, "must've had the star athlete's sixth sense that Marilyn was on a collision course with disaster." But it was not enough to save her.

Joe did not reenter Marilyn's life until after her divorce from Arthur Miller, in the difficult period before her death. One writer says the two got close enough to consider remarrying, and that Joe sent her his pajamas in the mail to let her know how he felt about it. Another book suggests that Joe, while being a boon to her in desperate times, was only a friend, one of the many who tried to help Marilyn find another route than suicide.

DiMaggio blamed Hollywood for killing his ex-wife, taking charge of her funeral and standing sentinel over it. When Marilyn's attorney complained that so many of her movie friends were being kept away, DiMaggio said, "If it weren't for those friends persuading her to stay in Hollywood, she would still be alive." To the last, and perhaps to this day, he maintained that Marilyn was just "a warm, big-hearted girl that everybody took advantage of."

DiMaggio has not remarried. Nor can he ever forget. At Marilyn's death he arranged to have fresh roses delivered to her grave site three times a week. Even after she was gone, he was sending her flowers.

Reflections on Billy

When, a month or so into the 1985 season, Billy Martin was hired to manage the Yankees for the fourth time, he was brought in to restore discipline to a club that, in the owner's view, had grown disrespectful of the rules and unconcerned whether it won or lost. Bringing Billy Martin in to restore respect for the rules had to be the sharpest of the many ironies that attended this situation, for throughout his playing and managing career Martin has teetered on the edge of being completely out of control. He is an outlaw demanding law and order. His drinking has led him to commit excessive acts. He tore apart his office in a bout of rage. His tirades against umpires have earned him numerous suspensions. As a player he went after opponents with his fists and, as a manager and grown man, he has ridiculed players on opposing teams, challenged them to fights, and exchanged blows after hours. He attacked a sportswriter and knocked him to the ground; afterward he was forced to pay a cash settlement and make a public apology. Billy Martin on discipline is like Ted Turner on good taste, or George Steinbrenner on fiscal restraint.

If Martin were not a great manager, combining tactical savvy with an acknowledged ability to inspire men, he probably would have been drummed out of the dugout a long time ago. People put up with him because he gets results—at least, one should add hastily, in the first year or two after he takes over a team. After that the fits of pique begin, the paranoia mounts, something happens—and out he goes, on to the next team, where the pattern reasserts itself. But you can't ever count Billy Martin out. Like an aging but crafty fighter, he keeps coming back, keeps jabbing, keeps ducking and rolling off the punches, determined to stay on his feet no matter what.

The boxing analogy is not original. In the public mind Billy *is* a fighter, a scrappy barroom brawler who will take on anybody, even the big guys, and lick 'em. Billy the Kid. Number One. Billy Brawl. Martin himself, with heavy doses of self-righteousness, likes to promote this image, and his pugilistic exploits, on and off the field, help back him up. That being the case, it may be possible to see his life as a single championship fight in which he battles a series of enemies, both personal and social, visible and invisible. Ring the bell, then, and let's have at it.

Round One:

Growing Up Billy

To get a clue why Billy Martin acts the way he does, go back to the beginning.

He was born May 16, 1928, under the sign of Taurus, the bull. His Christian name was Alfred Manuel Pesano. One book about him says that his father, a musician of Portuguese descent, left home before he was born, but in his autobiography Billy claims his mother kicked his dad out of the house because of certain indiscretions. The dominant figure in Martin's childhood was his mother, Jenny Downey, a strong-willed, pugnacious little woman whose own mother, it is said, would grab you and bite your hand if you said something she didn't like. Jenny Downey never forgave her husband for his skullduggery, and she swore that after he died she'd go to his funeral, pull up her dress, and "piss on his grave." She is now in her eighties and her son, needless to say, is immensely proud of her. He told reporters about a favorite button of hers that may fairly sum up her philosophy of life (and her son's): I'M ITALIAN. IF YOU DON'T LIKE IT, KISS MY ASS.

Billy grew up in tough West Berkeley, across the bay from San Francisco and eons away from the glitter and polish of the big city. The family was poor. Billy was raised by Jenny Downey and a stepfather. He reportedly had to share a bedroom with his grandmother until he was fifteen. Even as a kid he had to scramble for what he got and then fight to keep somebody from taking it away. "I grew up fighting," he told *Sports Illustrated*'s Ron Fimrite. "It isn't that I wanted to. It's just that I had no choice. These weren't kids who stole stuff. Their recreation was fighting."

Martin has said that his background—a Catholic up-bringing, his experience on the streets, knowing what it means to go without—has helped him get along with black and Hispanic ballplayers who also had tough childhoods. "When nothing talks to nothing," he has said, "they understand each other." While some may argue that Billy's relations with minorities have been less than ideal—the case of Reggie Jackson springs to mind—you cannot underestimate the effect of his childhood on all his later dealings with people, inside baseball and out. When you're challenged, you fight back. And if you're on the bottom, you fight back even harder. You fight dirty, you fight clean, you fight any way you need to in order to survive. Surviving is winning. Jenny Downey knew that. And her son Billy learned it.

Rounds Two, Three & Four:

The Early Fights

Almost from the first day he walked onto a major league ball field, Billy Martin was a marked man. Players and managers got to know him very quickly, and many disliked him. He was trouble.

One observer said the fiery, hot-tempered second baseman was "beset with all manner of actual and psychosomatic ailments—including hypertension, anxiety, insomnia and acute melancholia." It may be true there were more deep-seated reasons for Martin's behavior. Nevertheless, one should not overlook the simple fact of his aggressive loyalty to Casey Stengel. It was said that whenever the Yankees needed stirring up, Stengel, their manager, would tell his second baseman to go out and pick a fight with somebody. Martin loved Casey like a father. He would do anything for him, including risk possible suspension.

Whatever the motivation, Martin started getting into fights as soon as he donned Yankee pinstripes. Fists were the language that he apparently best understood. In his first full season in the majors, he duked it out with Jimmy Piersall, the Red Sox outfielder, before a game at Fenway Park. A couple months later he and Clint Courtney of the St. Louis Browns tangled in a game at Yankee Stadium. Courtney, whom Satchel Paige, a teammate, described as "the meanest man I know," must not have settled everything with Martin there, because they got into it again early the next season, in a bench-clearing brawl. The American League fined Courtney two hundred fifty dollars and Martin one hundred fifty for their part in the melee.

Not long after that, in July 1953, Martin was involved in another fight. This one was with Matt Batts, a catcher for the Tigers, but Billy pleaded innocent, claiming the other guy started it, not him. As Billy grows older this becomes an increasingly recognizable pattern—blame the other guy, it's the other guy's fault—but in this case, at least, he was right. Batts apologized and took responsibility for the incident.

Round Five
(Turning Point):

The Copa

For Billy Martin the player, the Copa was a catastrophe. It drove him from the protected grove, his major league home, and separated him from the best friends he would ever have and the only team he wanted to play on, the Yankees. Paradise (in his eyes) was lost, and the lessons he learned from it would stick with him for many, many years— if, indeed, they have ever left him.

The occasion was Martin's twenty-ninth birthday. A group of Yankees, including Martin, Mickey Mantle, Whitey Ford and Yogi Berra, went out to party at the Copacabana, a hopping New York City nightclub favored by celebrities. As with many historical events, the specific details of what occurred that night are difficult to ascertain precisely. Basically, it was something out of *Animal House*.

According to one account, Sammy Davis, Jr., was entertaining onstage. Some very large, very rowdy fellows, reputed to be members of a bowling team, insisted on yelling racial epithets at Sammy and, in general, made it impossible for the rest of the audience to enjoy the show. Their rudeness offended the finely tuned sensibilities of the Yankee ballplayers, who kindly asked the bowlers to shut their faces. When the bowlers ungraciously declined the offer, the festivities commenced. Mickey Mantle was quoted as saying he doesn't remember who threw the first punch. Quite likely no one else does, either. Bottles flew, wild punches were thrown, weapons came out. A fight even broke out in the cloakroom. Billy Martin, as usual, was somewhere in the center of things. When the last bits of glass had been swept up and all the blame assigned, the Yankees involved got hit with thousands of dollars in fines, and Martin, who paid a thousand by himself, was winging off to Kansas City in a seven-player deal.

"I cannot remember the exact year (I lost interest in baseball)," wrote the social columnist, Taki, in *Esquire* magazine, "but I do remember the precise moment. It was just after the Yankee management traded Billy Martin following the fracas at the old Copacabana nightclub. I was about twenty years old, and the realization that a fat man behind a desk is more important than a scrappy second baseman was traumatic indeed. I decided right then and there that, in general, businessmen were not to be trusted and, in particular, anyone who ran the Yankees was suspect from the start."

Billy Martin, the scapegoat of the affair, felt deeply betrayed. He cried when he heard he'd been traded. To him the Yankees were blood; to be cast out from them was to be cast out from family. The friendships he formed on that team—with Mickey Mantle, with Whitey Ford—were irreplaceable. They weren't merely his teammates, they were his brothers.

"I probably was the proudest Yankee of them all," Martin has said. "And I don't mean false pride. When it's real on a team it's a deep love-pride. There's nothing greater in the world than when somebody on the team does something good, and everybody gathers around to pat him on the back." After the Copacabana, the pats on the back turned to knives.

Round Six:

The Aftermath

If the Yankees were Billy Martin's family, Casey Stengel could be considered his father. Martin, the pint-sized son anxious to please, would run through a wall for Stengel if Casey asked him. He worshiped the old man and admired what he stood for on the Yankees and in baseball history, listening with his characteristic intensity to the master's game stratagems and advice. Later Martin would say, "Casey Stengel and Charlie Dressen were the two managers who taught me the most. The main difference was Casey always said 'We' and Charles always said 'I.'"

Stengel returned the compliments, calling Martin the

smartest little player he ever had. "If liking a kid who will never let you down in the clutch is favoritism," he said, "then I plead guilty." When some critics scoffed at Martin's prodigious .392 batting average in the minors in Phoenix, Stengel replied, "I don't care if he done it in Africa—it's still .392."

Together, the Stengel-Martin combination was respected around the league. After Martin rejoined the Yankees in 1955 following his hitch in the Army, Bill Corum, the sports columnist, wrote, "Until I arrived here in Chicago a few hours ago, I felt that, farfetched as it seemed, the perennial bridesmaids of the American League, the White Sox, might become bride. Now I know better. Because I picked up the paper and the headline said that Billy Martin had rejoined the Yankees. That, of course, just about settled the pennant race in the junior league . . . [because] you don't beat Stengel when he's got Billy Martin."

There remains some disagreement over how much of a part, if any, Stengel played in the Martin trade after the disastrous night at the Copa. If Casey had no active hand in it, one account says, he put up only passing resistance. For years afterward, goes this version, Martin would not speak to his old mentor, feeling that the loyalty he had shown for so long had not been returned.

In most contemporary accounts, including those of Martin and Mickey Mantle, the blame has focused on George Weiss, the authoritarian general manager of the Yankees. Weiss was the one who wanted Billy off the team, who felt he was a bad seed. The Copa was just an excuse to get rid of him, which Weiss had been angling to do for some time.

Another of Martin's supposed sins was the influence he exerted over Mickey Mantle, the Oklahoma country boy with the big home run swat. Nowadays, years after the fact, Mantle can laugh about it. "The Yankees always claimed they traded Billy because he was a bad influence on me," Mantle told Ron Fimrite. "Hell, they traded him in 1957, the year after I won the Triple Crown. Billy told George Weiss, our general manager, 'If I'm a bad influence, just look what

the guy did. How much better do you think he can get?'"
Mantle added with a chuckle, "Three years later, they found
it wasn't Billy who was the bad influence, anyway. It was
Whitey Ford."

Seen from a distance, the trade seems like fairly ordinary
fare—the lot of the major leaguer, now, then and forever-
more. Certainly Billy Martin is not the first nor the last
player to be ripped out of pleasant, familiar surroundings
and sent packing, to his own and to his fans' dismay. After
all, if Carlton Fisk can leave the Red Sox and Tom Seaver
can be dumped by the Mets, what's so special about Billy
and the Yankees?

Unfortunately, that's the long view, and Billy Martin has
never been able to take the long view on baseball or himself.
For him everything is of the moment, and matters absolutely. In his mind, he was picked on unfairly. He was betrayed—by whom, exactly, almost doesn't matter. He had
given everything to the Yankees, and they had rejected him.
If he did not know it already, Billy learned that baseball, like
any other business, was cutthroat. Sentiment went only so
far.

Another lesson was reinforced as well, one that his
mother, Jenny Downey, had taught him. Watch where you
put your trust. Be wary when dealing with those in power,
for they will cheat and deceive you. The young Billy Martin
would hold this lesson close in the years to come.

Round Seven:

Decline

Before the trade, Billy had actually become a pretty
good ballplayer. Very competitive. A Phil Garner type.

Good in the clutch, real tough around World Series time.

But Martin left his best years behind him in New York. His all-out play all the time led to a series of injuries that over his career diminished his time on the field. He became little more than a journeyman, bouncing from ballclub to ballclub. After the Yankees he never played in another World Series. His last stop was in Minnesota, a second-division team. It was an ignominious end for a man who detested losing and puffed up with a rooster's pride over being known as a *Yankee,* back when the term meant something.

Yet, even in other uniforms, Billy was still Billy. In 1960, the year before he retired, he broke Jim Brewer's jaw with a punch after the Cubs pitcher brushed him back with a fastball. When Brewer and the Cubs announced they were suing him for over a million dollars, Martin said, "How do they want it, by cash or check?" He was suspended and fined for the incident, and years later his victim, Jim Brewer, was awarded ten thousand dollars in damages.

Round Eight:

Return

As Billy moved into managing, where he has gained far more personal success than he ever did as a second baseman, his career began to look more and more like Boom Boom Mancini's. Who was Billy knocking down now? You needed a scorecard to keep track.

While managing the Twins, he rushed out of a Detroit restaurant to break up a fight between Bob Allison and Dave Boswell, teammates under Martin at Minnesota. Boswell, a pitcher, had Allison, an outfielder–first baseman, helpless on the ground and was kicking him in the side. On Martin's arrival, Boswell turned on him and (according to Billy) struck him hard in the temple and chest. But poor Dave never took lessons on the streets of Berkeley, California. He didn't know what hit him. Martin came at him like Sugar Ray Leonard and, as Billy recalled, peppered him with "about five or six punches in the stomach, and a couple to the head, and when Boswell came off the wall, I hit him again. He was out before he hit the ground."

The Twins won their division that year, in Martin's first try at managing, but Billy got the ax anyway. Some observers believed that the front office disgruntlement with Martin stemmed from his habit of drinking with his players. After the Twins came a stormy, if successful, tenure with Detroit, highlighted by Martin allegedly ordering his pitchers to throw spitballs in response to flagrant violations of the spitter rule by Gaylord Perry. Martin was suspended for that one.

"I'd fire my mother for the chance to hire Billy Martin," said Texas owner Bob Short, who got his chance after the Tigers dumped him near the end of the 1973 season. With the Rangers it was more of the same. Billy was knocked on his butt during a wild rhubarb with the Cleveland Indians, and then, in an outburst Martin later apologized for, he slapped the face of the team's male traveling secretary. After a nasty shouting match with new Rangers owner Brad Corbett, Billy was gone from Texas too. "My differences with Billy were a culmination of many things over a period of time," Corbett told the press, speaking for all owners everywhere who've hired and fired Martin.

A record like this might already be enough for most men, but Billy was just getting started. He had one aim in life, and that was to get back home to his beloved Yankees. The cycle was completed in August 1975, shortly after the Rangers fired him. "This has got to be one of my biggest thrills," he said at the time his new job as manager of the New York Yankees was announced. Little did he know. His new owner: George Steinbrenner.

Rounds Nine
Through Thirteen:

The Yankees
and All That

It was in New York, in his various and bloody managerial stints with the Yankees, that the public perception of Billy Martin took firm hold. Baseball fans knew about him already, but it was here, in America's media capital, along with George and Reggie and The Best Team Money Can Buy, that those outside of baseball discovered Billy Martin. Many weren't sure how to react.

- ITEM: His near-fight with George Steinbrenner in Yankee training camp before one season.
- ITEM: His famous, nationally televised spat with Reggie Jackson in the dugout during a game against the Red Sox. A livid Martin accused Jackson of not hustling after a ball and almost delivered a haymaker to his chops.
- ITEM: His angry quarrel with Thurman Munson in Chicago's O'Hare Airport that nearly developed into a fistfight.
- ITEM: The seemingly endless stream of insults, locker-room arguments, shouting matches and the like with his players. The Yankees in this period were, in Jim Murray's words, "a traveling dock fight," and Martin was a prime instigator.

Out of this maelstrom, the public came to know Billy and, for the most part, liked what it saw. Most appealing was the little-guy aspect of his personality. He was one guy not afraid to stick up for his rights, to stand up to the bullies of the world. This is the Billy you see on the Lite Beer commercials: the feisty yet engaging little man, the cowboy and scrapper who can still poke fun at himself.

Certainly, Billy benefited from the fact that his two principal adversaries on the Yankees were largely perceived as ghouls: George Steinbrenner, the rich, string-pulling businessman with the Woody Hayes mentality and the suffocatingly overbearing management style; and Reggie Jackson who, as Tom Boswell has noted, could make you want to repeal the Bill of Rights if he talked long enough in favor of it. All America loves an underdog, and they apparently found one in Billy Martin. Billy vs. George. Billy vs. Reggie. Billy vs. Reggie and George. Appearing in Detroit just after he chewed Reggie out in that televised Boston game, Martin received a standing ovation. The dramatic 1978 announcement at an old-timer's game that the then-deposed Martin would be returning to manage the team was met by tears of joy at Yankee Stadium. Martin today remains a highly popular figure.

Beyond his surface appeal as underdog, Billy is a much more complex—and troubling—figure. "First I'm a man, then I'm a manager," he says in his best macho-speak, and the way he must prove it, even into his fifties, is by fighting. The man, in many important ways, is an adolescent, ready at all times to jump bad at perceived violations of his turf.

Before taking over as Yankee manager a second time, Martin beat up a Nevada sportswriter who later demanded and got a public apology and cash settlement from him. Martin claimed at first that he didn't start it, that the writer had goaded him. "I don't want to fight you. Little kids fight. Men don't fight," he supposedly told him.

The sportswriter, Roy Hagar, saw it differently. Martin, he said, was berating a group of writers and then ordered him to give up his notes.

"I said, 'I'm sorry, I can't do that.' He said it again and I put my hands behind my back with my notebook. I knew something was going to happen. Everybody sort of started crowding in," Hagar recalled.

Hagar continued, "He looked away for a second, then hit me in the teeth. The first punch rocked my head off and knocked my glasses off. Then he hit me in the right eye and that was the punch that was most painful. Then I got up and said, 'Look, I don't want to fight you.' I put my hands out and tried to hold his. He said something and he hit me again. That punch would have floored me, but it knocked me into a table and broke my fall. I asked where my glasses were, and someone gave them to me. I saw my notes on the floor. I had gone that far to protect them, so I grabbed them, got my coat and left."

Added Hagar, "He [Martin] was the quickest guy I've ever been in a fight with. He hit me before I knew it. I didn't even get a punch in."

Round Fourteen:

Of Marshmallows and Men

To be Billy Martin is to be a perpetual target. One reason, of course, is his combative managerial style. If Rommel, the Nazi panzer commander, had been in baseball, he would have managed like Billy Martin. Not only do Martin's teams beat their opponents on a ball field, they show them up. Double steals, the suicide squeeze, an emphasis on fundamentals, psychological warfare—these are all integral elements of the Martin attack. He is also not above trickery. A classic Martin ploy is to have a runner feign a stumble off first base and draw a throw, while the man on third scores.

Off the field, Billy has made plenty of enemies as well. His beer commercials, with their lighthearted references to his prowess as a fighter, have only solidified his reputation. No doubt lots of people come looking for Billy when he's in town: It's easy to envision the local Joe Palooka, with three or four shots of Jack Daniels under his belt, looking to impress his girlfriend or the guys at work by picking a fight with the famous Billy Martin. So it may very well be that the marshmallow salesman Billy punched out in that Bloomington, Minnesota, hotel was eager for trouble, that he stepped over the line and No. 1 was merely protecting himself, as anyone would do.

All in all, you'd be more willing to give Martin the benefit of the doubt in some of these cases if it weren't for the attitude of wounded innocence he invariably adopts, like the cat caught with a feather in its mouth after the pet parakeet has disappeared. After the Bloomington incident Martin said, probably fighting back a sniffle, "I'm not a violent person."

Not a violent person? Come on, Billy, what kind of saps do you take us for? What about that office you tore up when you were managing the A's? Did the chairs throw themselves against the walls? And what about that scuffle with Ed Whitson toward the end of the '85 season?

Then again, Billy may actually believe that he isn't prone to violence—that he is, after all, only a victim. Perhaps, in those internal dialogues of the self in which even baseball managers must engage, he really does see himself as the injured party, unjustly accused. Which brings us to the last round and to Billy's final foe—the implacable enemy that has worked against him in all the previous rounds, and the foe over which he must ultimately triumph.

Round Fifteen:

Himself

The business of analyzing Billy Martin is a popular one among baseball writers and close observers of the scene. What makes him behave so badly? Everyone seems to have an opinion.

Many blame it on the bottle and point out that many of the incidents that have marred his career have occurred while he was drinking. This may be so, but it still does not answer the more fundamental questions of what drives Billy, what pushes him so hard, what makes him such a creature of excess.

Some resort to the language of the poet to explain Billy. Donald Hall, the poet and critic who has written a great deal about baseball, calls Martin "combative, self-justified, vigorous, vulgar, shrewd, streetwise, self-pitying and scandalous. Shakespeare might have invented him, as an inversion of Hotspur—a mock-heroic figure with Ancient Pistol's braggadocio and Falstaff's gregariousness." Translated, Hall likes Billy's moxie.

But others consider his antics nothing more than macho bluster, a craving for attention from a woefully insecure ego. Geoffrey Stokes of the *Village Voice* cites his "apparently inescapable loss of control. Every game in which Martin and his teams are able to control chance within the boundaries of the playing field leaves him more vulnerable to the breakdown when off-field events remind him how little control he really has."

Dr. Carol Tavris, author of a widely read study of anger,

warned parents on television about their children's temper tantrums. "You have to be careful that you don't give in to them each time, and let them think they can gain something by throwing their tantrums, or they'll grow up to be Billy Martin," she said. It seems the course of baseball history would have been changed irrevocably if only someone had applied the palm more often and with greater vigor to baby Billy's bare ass.

The simplest theory about Martin may be the best. He's a kid who never grew up. As an adult he settled arguments the same way he did when young—by punching the other guy's lights out. Like the ninety-eight-pound weakling who got sand kicked in his face and sent away for the Charles Atlas body-building handbook, Billy never forgot—and always got even.

Lowell Cohn, columnist for the *San Francisco Chronicle* and the best of the Martinologists, writes, "Billy never learned how to get along. You knew kids like that when you went to grade school. They were always fighting, and the teacher was sticking them in the back of the class, and that made them fight even more.

"Billy is like that kid. Emotionally, he is a twisted twelve-year-old. He is suspicious and cruel, and gloom hangs around him like a bad odor. For some reason, he is in emotional pain—he probably has been for as long as he's been conscious of the world—and nothing he ever did, not drinking himself blind or sneak-punching enemies or managing the Yankees, ever drove the ache away."

4
Those Brooklyn Dodgers: The Team That Will Not Die

"What is it then between us?
What is the count of the scores or
    hundreds of years between us?
Whatever it is, it avails not—
    distance avails not, and place
    avails not,
I too lived, Brooklyn of ample hills
    was mine."

—WALT WHITMAN, former
    Brooklyn resident

1
Why Brooklyn?

IN THE 1950s Brooklyn, New York, was a crazy, boisterous, roiling city, and the craziest place to be was Ebbets Field at game time, Ebbets, the home of the Dodgers,
seated thirty-two thousand people, but for a big game they
could squeeze in another five thousand. They led the league
in attendance in Brooklyn usually, and the fans didn't need
paid clowns like the Phillie Fanatic or the San Diego
Chicken to help them make noise. They had plenty of homegrown fanatics in Brooklyn, and they all worked for free.

Before a game many of the fans at Ebbets would wait in
line to shake the hand of their favorite Dodger players.
After that they'd get down to the un-serious business of
creating a ruckus. Dozens of people brought hand-painted
signs, others dressed up in goofy costumes.

Ebbets Field was a rolling, palpitating field of color and
noise, always noise. People yelled themselves hoarse by the
third inning; the smart ones brought whistles and blew on
them when they weren't yelling. Hilda Chester, ordered not
to yell by her doctor because of her heart condition, banged
on a frying pan or rang a cowbell. The Dodger Sym-Phony, a
five-man fruitcake band featuring a trombone, trumpet,
snare drum, bass drum and clashing cymbals, added to the
cacophony.

Loyal and loud back then, Brooklyn fans haven't
changed a bit over the years. They still talk about their
heroes, still follow them even though nearly three decades
have passed since the Dodgers last fielded a team in
Brooklyn. The Bums, it seems, refuse to die. They've been

celebrated in poetry and song and numerous books. There is a small but persistent market for Brooklyn memorabilia today—pennants, caps, old photos, buttons. A Brooklyn Dodger Hall of Fame has even been formed.

When the Dodgers left for Los Angeles in the late fifties, their arch-rivals, the New York Giants, moved to San Francisco. Both teams departed amid great controversy and bitterness, vestiges of which pop up from time to time in New York. When New York Telephone announced that Brooklyn was getting a new area code—distinct from Manhattan and the Bronx—the author Norman Mailer, a resident of Brooklyn Heights, fumed, "This is the worst thing to happen since the Dodgers left town."

Before the start of one recent baseball season, Bob McGee, a freelance writer, stood in a Los Angeles building overlooking Dodger Stadium and recorded his impressions for *The New York Times*. "The window reflected my rueful look," he wrote. "And I wondered why the Brooklyn Dodgers couldn't have been given the Long Island Rail Road station site at the junction of Atlantic and Flatbush to replace Ebbets Field. Today, that site stands as a monument to nothingness . . ."

This fan loyalty spills over into arguments of a baseball nature. Sparky Anderson created a minor furor in the New York media a few years ago by claiming that his 1976 Big Red Machine—Morgan, Rose, Bench, Foster, Concepcion, et al.—was a better team than Brooklyn in the fifties. What, better than *our* boys? What are you, nuts, Sparky? The New York media wouldn't stand for such heresy.

This is indeed a curious phenomenon, not wholly explained by the popular bent for nostalgia. Does anyone pine for the old Washington Senators? The St. Louis Browns? Uh, the Seattle Pilots? To be fair, these aren't entirely comparable situations. Seattle eventually got the Mariners to replace the woeful Pilots, and St. Louis still had the Cardinals after the Browns straggled out of town. Some holdouts may still fondly remember the Senators, but it's nothing like with the Dodgers. And there continues to be talk about restoring baseball to D.C., so nostalgia for the Senators may be tempered by the expectation on the part of fans in the area of getting another major league club sometime in the future.

That will never happen in Brooklyn. The city has changed, the country has changed. This must be at the core of the continuing appeal of the team: The Brooklyn Dodgers will never come back. They're gone for good.

It's logical that New Yorkers would feel protective about their late Dodgers, but in another respect it doesn't make much sense at all. In a city that prides itself on its hipness and sophistication, why do people hang onto this tattered little ragamuffin ballclub of the past? It's like learning Donald Trump sleeps with a teddy bear.

The Giants had a long, colorful history in New York too, but they don't engender the loyalty that Brooklyn does. So why this loving attachment to the Bums? Why do so many tough, no-nonsense individuals still cling sentimentally to a team that hasn't played a game in decades? These seem questions deserving further investigation.

2
The Early Days

Most contemporary accounts of the Brooklyn franchise tend to concentrate on the club's successful years, skimming over the far lengthier period when the team was merely rotten. This is a mistake, like telling the story of the '69 Miracle Mets without mentioning '62 or '63, the sad-sack beginning years of the franchise. If all a ballclub did was win, what fun would that be? Without the Marv Throneberrys and Pumpsie Greens, the later victory of the Seavers and Jerry Koosmans would not have been nearly as sweet. It was the same with Brooklyn, an orphan of a ballclub that grew up to challenge—and whip—the big kids on the block. You can't neglect this aspect of the team's appeal. They were losers that made good.

Brooklyn at the turn of the century was crisscrossed by trolley car lines. Fans who came out to the ballgame had to Dodge trolleys to get into the park, and the team became known as the "Trolley Dodgers," later shortened to "Dodgers." The term was a derogatory one, which seems fitting considering the early checkered history of the franchise. For many, many years the Dodgers stunk.

They earned their nickname of "Bums" on merit. Though nowadays the appellation has a rosy, sentimental quality about it, Brooklyn fans bestowed it with the angry resentment and hurt pride that anyone who has lived and died with a losing ballclub knows all too well. The team really was a bunch of bums, seldom getting out of the second division and just barely escaping the cellar year after year. A couple times they shocked baseball (and themselves) by actually winning the pennant, but after both of those seasons the Bums reverted to form and dipped into the second division the next year. Their position at or near the bottom of the National League was so entrenched that a sportswriter, seeing the team creep up to an unfamiliar place in the standings, warned that "overconfidence may cost the Dodgers sixth place."

The man who led the Brooklyners through this desert of second-division finishes was Wilbert Robinson, their manager. Known as "Uncle Robbie" for his folksy, genial air, he set the tone and style for the team. He was a bit of a boob. Intending to give the ump at home plate the lineup card, he instead handed over his laundry list. Supposedly he wouldn't start players whose names he couldn't spell; other Dodgers didn't play because he forgot they were on the team. When three of his baserunners ended up on third base in a game, Uncle Robbie yelled, "Leave them alone. That's the first time they've been together all year!"

In the late twenties and early thirties, at the close of Robinson's long tenure as manager, people gave the Dodgers another nickname to describe their play on the field: "The Daffiness Boys." They featured players like

Babe Herman, who caught fly balls with his head. Clyde Day, a pitcher from Pea Ridge, Arkansas, made pig noises after striking a batter out. Boom-Boom Beck got his nickname because bats went "boom-boom" every time he pitched. Another mainstay of the pitching staff was Luke "Hot Potato" Hamlin, who, it was said, was so wild that if he jumped off the Brooklyn Bridge, he would not hit water.

One of the orneriest of the old Dodgers was Van Lingle Mungo, the man with the lyrical name and wild fastball. After a game in which Dodger outfielder Tom Winsett muffed a fly ball that cost Mungo a win, the enraged right-hander charged off the field and fired off a telegram to his wife back home in South Carolina: "Pack your bags and come to Brooklyn, honey. If Winsett can play in the big leagues, it's a cinch you can too."

Van Lingle was a battler whose temper got him into fights with both opponents and teammates. "Mungo and I get along fine," Casey Stengel remarked. "I just tell him I won't stand for no nonsense—and then I duck."

Let us not forget Casey. He was there too, he put in his time. He broke in with the Dodgers as a player and then, in his first go at managing, led the team to three consecutive second-division finishes in the mid-thirties. Red Smith wrote, "It is erroneous and unjust to conceive of Casey Stengel merely as a clown. He is something else entirely—a competitor who always had fun competing, a fighter with a gift of laughter." Well and truly put, but it should be noted nevertheless that Casey's most memorable stunt, letting a sparrow fly out from under his cap, occurred in a game at Ebbets Field, home of the Brooklyn Dodgers.

3
Respectability

With the coming of Larry MacPhail, a hard-driving businessman, the age of respectability dawned. In 1938 the phone company cut off service at the Dodger offices for failure to pay its bills. In debt up to its ears, the club was in danger of folding.

Larry MacPhail, hired as president, turned the team around. He borrowed money and wheeled and dealed, bringing in Red Barber to call the games on radio, ordering the renovation of old, shopworn Ebbets Field and the installation of lights, revamping the farm system, and putting resources and energy into player development. Results were almost immediate. In 1939, with Leo Durocher as manager, the Dodgers rose like some great amphibious creature out of their accustomed depths in the second division and finished third. Two years later they won the pennant, and the overhaul was complete.

This was obviously quite a change from past Brooklyn performances, and one that their long-suffering fans rejoiced in. Yet more than just the win-loss columns changed in Brooklyn. Under Larry MacPhail, the Dodgers got down to business. The Daffiness Boys were rooted out, and in their stead came careerists, both in the office and on the field. This movement accelerated in the years to come under Branch Rickey and reached its apotheosis with Walter O'Malley, who sought to fill his club with men who conformed to his image of what a ballplayer should be. Here, in fact, are the origins of the squeaky-clean Dodger image and management philosophy that continues, under the ownership of the O'Malley family, in Los Angeles. It was also this O'Malley way of doing business that rankled—and enraged—so many New Yorkers after the team left town.

4
The Dodger Who Ran Into Walls

One of the greatest of all the Brooklyn Dodgers was a man whose youthful exuberance and spirited play nearly destroyed him. The same qualities that singled him out on a ball field—his optimism and energy, the joy he got from playing—wrecked his career. "I'm a firm believer in positive thinking," he said. "I used to stand out there in center field and say to myself, 'Hit it to me, hit it to me.' Every pitch, I wanted that ball." He wanted that ball so much he risked his life to get it. His name was Pete Reiser.

Reiser was a natural. Many observers, including Branch Rickey, described him as the best young ballplayer they had ever seen. Scouted by the major leagues at age twelve, he led the National League in hitting at twenty-two. He was a switch-hitter. After he broke his right arm, he taught himself to throw left-handed. He played third base and the outfield, where he was as fast as anybody in the game. Leo Durocher said, "Willie Mays had everything. Pete Reiser had everything but luck."

In a game in the summer of 1942, Enos Slaughter of the Cardinals hit a rising liner deep into center. Reiser, playing center field, set off in pursuit. Either forgetting about or ignoring the existence of the unpadded Ebbets Field walls, he smashed full-speed into the wall and dropped to the ground as if felled by a sniper's bullet. "It felt like a hand grenade went off inside my head," he said later.

The ball trickled from his glove, and the opportunistic Slaughter raced for an inside-the-park homer. The blow gave Reiser a concussion and fractured his skull. Carried off the field on a stretcher, he remarkably found his way back into the lineup only three days later. He pinch-hit and got a single. As he rounded first, he passed out.

"Pistol Pete"

After an accident like that you would expect Reiser to come back a wiser, more cautious player. He did not. "His weakness," said Red Smith, "was there never was a ballpark large enough to contain his effort." Like a horse that loves to gallop, Reiser could not contain himself—could not accept his own limits or the simple physical limits of the arenas in which he played. More to the point is teammate Cookie Lavagetto's assessment: "Pete had one failing—he never knew where the hell the walls were."

Outfield walls today are padded because of Reiser's headlong spirit. He had to be carried off the field on a stretcher numerous times after collisions. After making a spectacular catch in a game, Reiser hit the wall and then the ground. Unsure whether the ball had stayed in Pete's mitt, the second-base umpire had to run out to center to make the call. The batter was out. And so was Pete. He left the game flat on his back.

In 1947, after he returned from World War II, a wall nearly killed him. "All ballplayers have a great amount of inner conceit, and it has to be used," he said once. "Every hitter thinks he's the world's greatest hitter; every pitcher thinks he's the world's greatest pitcher. To be great ballplayers, they have to think that all the time." Reiser had that inner conceit and that inner conceit told him he could get the ball Pirate outfielder Culley Rikard hit over his head.

Pete did get it but he hit the center field wall at Ebbets on a dead run. When he woke up, he was in the hospital. He couldn't move, his legs were paralyzed—a condition that lasted over a week. After being released from the hospital he came back for the rest of the season, but the collision effectively finished him as a full-time player. He complained of grogginess in the field and the Dodgers benched him. He was twenty-eight at the time, coming into what should have been his prime. Still able to hit well, he hung around the majors for another five years, then became a coach and minor league manager.

With failure, comes blame. Since Reiser did not turn out to be the ballplayer everyone expected, some people blamed

Leo Durocher, his first manager in the majors. Seeing what a wild outfielder Pete was, they said, Leo should have put him permanently at third base, where he was safe. Others put the onus on Dodger management for bringing Pete back too quickly from his injuries. Reiser himself blamed no one. "Every time I hit a wall, I was going for a drive that meant the ballgame," he said in his defense.

What probably wrecked Reiser, after all, was himself. What made him great also proved his undoing. Frank Howard, who played under Reiser in the minors, remembers his former manager as being "very, very intense. He used to say to me over and over, 'Eliminate doubt, eliminate doubt.'"

There was no letting up for Reiser when he played, no easing off the pedal. This intensity, coupled with the absence of doubt, brought him to his knees. The walls told him no, yet he would not listen. He got up and ran into another. His was a fool's errand, but of a kind with which we can sympathize. What one of us has not, like hardheaded Pete, run up against walls that wouldn't bend to our wishes?

5
Rivalries

Pete Reiser's career as a Dodger spans a transition period for the Brooklyn franchise as a whole. He joined the team as it was getting respectable, and left it in the late forties as it was entering its period of greatness. Replacing him in center field was rifle-armed Carl Furillo, who moved to right with the emergence of Duke Snider. With Snider, the pieces were falling into place.

Another transitional figure is Leo Durocher who, save for the year of his suspension, managed the club until midseason of 1948. Leo was, in Dick Young's words, "a pop-off guy": a pool shark, a streetwise gambler with suspected mob connections, a nightclubber and a clothes dandy, a bench jockey of the most vulgar type, a publicity hound, a friend of the fast-track Hollywood crowd. While with the Dodgers, Brooklyn fans could forgive The Lip his every excess. But what they could never forgive was Leo leaving the Dodgers to go over to the crosstown New York Giants. Not until Walter O'Malley ripped the world out from under their feet did Brooklyn fans find a villain to surpass Leo.

The antagonism Brooklyn fans felt for the traitorous Durocher was real, though it may seem curious in this day of diluted baseball rivalries. In either league, the game's best rivalries today consist of teams from different cities or states; New York–Boston is perhaps the most notable. Though local or intercity rivalries—Yankees–Mets, Cubs–White Sox, A's–Giants—flourish, they can only play for keeps in the World Series.

Not so with the old Giants and Dodgers. They faced off regularly during the season, and often in tight, excruciatingly tense games late in the year when both teams were in the pennant hunt. Unlike modern rivalries, in which the sheer distances prevent most fans from seeing their teams play on the road, Dodger fans needed only a subway token to see their boys take on the Jints at the Polo Grounds. A trip of this kind was not undertaken lightly, though. There were fans on both sides who would brain you with a bottle if they saw you rooting against their team. A good Giant-Dodger game was a blood drama with the passion and fire of a Latin American soccer match.

Their most famous scrap came in 1951, when Bobby Thomson hit the home run that beat the Dodgers in the playoffs. Brooklyn fans mourn this date the way people mourned the death of Roosevelt. Carl Erskine, who threw the pitch the Giant third baseman hit, said, "That's the first time I've seen a big fat wallet go flying into the seats." Roy Campanella, watching the ball fly out of the park, kept repeating to himself, "Sink, you devil, sink." Jackie Robinson said, "One minute we're in the World Series, the next minute we're in the shithouse." And Dick Young, implying that the Dodgers had choked again in the clutch, wrote, "The tree that grows in Brooklyn is an apple tree."

But, in a curious way, a loss of this magnitude adds to rather than subtracts from our esteem for those Dodgers. They lost mightily and with heroic splendor. They weren't made of stainless steel like their other crosstown rivals, the Yankees. They could be beaten, and in the most heartbreaking fashion. Bobby Thomson beat them with a homer in the ninth inning of the third game of the playoffs. The Phillies nosed them out for the pennant on the last day of the season. They took the invincible Yankees to seven in the Series, yet still they got beat. They seemed in a battle not only with opposing ballclubs, but with fate.

Adding still more zest to this Promethean struggle was the character of the men on the field. They were, as Roger Kahn wrote, "a fascinating mix of vigorous men." Most fascinating of all was the second baseman, a pivotal figure in American life in the twentieth century. This aspect of the allure of the old Dodgers cannot be overstated. When you were in the seats at Ebbets Field watching Jackie Robinson play, you weren't just watching a baseball game, you were sitting in on history.

6
Jackie and Branch

Baseball was the sport around which post-war America revolved, and when a twenty-eight-year-old black man broke the color barrier in the major leagues and came to play (and stay, man, *stay!*) for the Dodgers, it shook up the whole country, setting off a political and social revolution that is still going on. Came Jackie Robinson; then came Rosa Parks, *Brown* v. *The Board of Education,* Little Rock, the march from Selma, the 1965 Civil Rights Voting Act.

The story of how baseball got off the plantation ought to be told over and over again, lest anyone forget what Jackie Robinson had to go through just to play ball. The fights he walked away from, the insults he took, the threats to his life, the pettinesses and slights that must've been so demeaning to a man of his pride and intelligence, the fastballs aimed at his head, the relentless, unyielding pressure he faced from the day he first put on spikes for the Montreal Royals, the Dodger farm club where he broke in. The writer Jimmy Cannon called Robinson in those first painful years "the loneliest man I've ever seen," an irony of considerable strength when you realize that Jackie was one of the most watched men in America. He carried the hopes and dreams of millions on his back, just as countless other bilious souls wished him dead. It took the patience and fortitude of a saint to do what Jackie did and indeed, as the years roll by, that is what he is in danger of becoming. Jackie Robinson, the saint. Jackie Robinson, the icon.

This is an understandable trend, but one that ought not to go unchallenged. Robinson was not a saint; he was a man, full of contradictions. After his groundbreaking other blacks joined him in the majors, and the idea of black big leaguers became somewhat less inflammatory. The big battle over, Jackie could be more himself and less the torchbearer. Himself was nobody to mess with, a fearsome, bust-your-ass competitor.

He could go from first to third on a sacrifice bunt. In a game against the Giants he laid a bunt down the first base line, and as the ball rolled foul and the pitcher stooped over to pick it up, Robinson ran right over him. "This guy didn't just come to play," Leo Durocher said. "He come to beat ya. He come to stuff the goddamn bat right up your ass."

Another story about Robinson the competitor is worth telling, though it probably won't make the history textbooks. At this time Leo Durocher, managing the Giants, had just married the actress Laraine Day. The Giants and Dodgers were squared off against each other and Robinson was at the plate. From the dugout, Durocher screamed, "My dick to you, Robinson!"

Jackie stepped out of the box, gazing over at Leo. "Give it to Laraine," he said. "She needs it more than I do."

The other half of baseball's historic civil rights tandem, though not as celebrated as the warrior who did it on the field, has deservedly achieved folk hero status in his own right. First you see it, then you do it—and Branch Rickey was the one to see it. Beyond this, he possessed the practical force to put his vision of fairness and equality into effect.

The best one-word description of Rickey may be "canny." More so than any of his contemporaries, he understood the value of baseball horseflesh; Ray Kennedy called him the wiliest negotiator this side of an Arab slave market. "Keep your mouth shut, your hands in your pocket, and don't drink" was the common advice for any ballplayer who talked contract with him.

Rickey would let loose cannon peals of polysyllabic oratory, and then hide behind the smoke. Chuck ("The Rifleman") Connors, who played briefly in the majors before quitting to become a TV actor, heard Rickey give a speech in spring training one year. "I heard him talk for an hour and a half on how to take a lead at first base, and he never got the runner more than ten feet off the bag," Connors recalled. After denying a raise to a Brookyn aide, Rickey consoled him, "Remember, young fellow. Happiness always lurks close to a poor man." "Yeah, that's the trouble," replied the glum aide. "It lurks and lurks and lurks."

Rickey was color-blind except for green. After leaving the Dodgers he went to the front office of the Pirates, a last place club. When Ralph Kiner asked him for a raise after leading the league in home runs the previous year, he said, "We could have finished last without you." Later Rickey said about his future Hall of Famer, "I don't want to sell Ralph, but if something overwhelming comes along, I'm willing to be overwhelmed."

The boss man got a comeuppance of sorts at a reunion of the 1934 St. Louis Cardinals, the famed Gashouse Gang that Rickey, as vice president and general manager, helped assemble. Speaking at the banquet, Rickey praised the team as men who loved the game so much they would have played for nothing. At which point Pepper Martin stood up and said, "Thanks to you, Mr. Rickey, we almost did."

Like Jackie Robinson, Branch Rickey has undergone a process of idealization since his death; he is seen nowadays as a great humanitarian and a fighter for justice and fair play. He was certainly all of that, and the sharpest of businessmen too. He could not let things go to waste; everyone had a job to do, and that job was to utilize resources in the most efficient, cost-effective manner possible. In plain terms, what Branch Rickey saw in Jackie Robinson and the players of the Negro Leagues was a resource being wasted. That offended Rickey, and he put those young men to work.

7
The Golden Years

In the late forties and fifties the Dodgers fielded a Hall of Fame lineup that, overall, stacks up favorably against any in baseball history. They won a handful of pennants in their time but, owing to the unfriendly whims of destiny, only one World Championship. They had the misfortune of playing in the same era with an even greater team, Casey Stengel's New York Yankees.

A roll call of the old Brooklyn lineup:

> **First Base:** Gil Hodges. The Gibraltar of the Dodgers. Decent, solid, a Lou Gehrig figure. While Hodges suffered through a terrible World Series batting slump, a Brooklyn priest instructed his congregation, "It's too hot for a sermon. Keep the commandments and pray for Gil Hodges."
> **Second Base:** Jackie Robinson.

Shortstop: Pee Wee Reese. "A captain among men," as Red Barber said.

At the end of World War II, Navyman Reese was on board a battleship cruising off the waters near Guam when his Chief Petty Officer informed him of the signing of a new Dodger recruit—a black man who was expected to play in the majors.

"Is that a fact?" said Pee Wee, mildly curious.

"Pee Wee," said the officer somberly. "He's a shortstop."

"Oh shit," Pee Wee said.

Pee Wee need not have worried. He was too good to be moved off his position, even by the great Jackie Robinson. Reese, too, advanced the cause of integration simply by playing alongside Jackie and teaming with him to anchor the center of the infield. The symbolism was unavoidable: black and white, working together and getting results. Before Robinson entered the majors, Dixie Walker and some other Dodgers circulated a petition asking Branch Rickey not to bring a colored man onto the team. A Kentuckian by birth, Pee Wee Reese refused to sign the petition, and the New South was born.

Third Base: Billy Cox. Not of the caliber of his infield mates, but still noteworthy. A glove man. He weighed a hundred fifty pounds and all of it, they said, was heart.

Featured Performance by a Left Fielder in a Continuing Series: Sandy Amoros. Amoros was the hero of the seventh game of the 1955 World Series, the only one the Brooklyners would ever win. The Havana, Cuba, native prevented yet another crunching Yankee defeat of the Dodgers by making a terrific one-handed grab of a drive by Yogi Berra down the left field line. Asked how he made the catch, Amoros said, "I dunno. I just run like hell."

Center Field: Duke Snider. The golden boy of the team. He came from California, but the Brooklyn fans didn't hold that against him. "Oh, the unruffled non-chalance of that game!" wrote Philip Roth in *Portnoy's Complaint,* in tribute to the way The Duke trotted in from the outfield after making an inning-ending catch, stepping down on the second base bag and tossing the ball, "with just a flick of the wrist," to the opposing team's shortstop as he came onto the field.

The man certainly had flair, not to mention the kind of power that blasted balls out of Ebbets Field onto adjacent Bedford Avenue. Very athletic, very emotional and expressive, Snider was a Gene Kelly type, as opposed to the Astaire-like classicism of a Joe DiMaggio.

Right Field: Carl Furillo's spot. Though a gifted player, Furillo serves today mainly as foreground to the more famous object he protected: HIT SIGN, WIN SUIT. This sign, four feet high by forty feet long, sat at the base of the scoreboard at Ebbets, some four hundred feet from home. With Furillo and friends guarding it, you needed a grenade launcher to hit the sign. But with this piece of promotional genius, Abe Stark, the Brooklyn shop owner whose firm it advertised, earned himself a permanent niche in New York City lore. Who Abe Stark was and what his sign said are trivia questions every New Yorker should get.

Catcher: Roy Campanella. His marvelous career abbreviated by a crippling car wreck, Campanella "is an example of what man can do if he refuses to quit," said former president Dwight D. Eisenhower. Branch Rickey said Campy was that rare person who possesses "humility without affectation and strength without rancor."

Asked by Roger Kahn if he had any bitterness over what had happened to him, Campy answered a flat no. "I tell ya," he said, "hate don't get you nowhere. Don't keep hate stirring down inside."

Pitchers: To name but three of the more colorful ones:

Joe Black, who had an overpowering fastball before he threw his arm out, toured the country talking to people about his teammate Jackie Robinson, and later served as an usher at the funeral of Martin Luther King, Jr. The Yankees' Johnny Mize hit a big home run off Black in a Series game, breaking up a shutout. Wrote John Drebinger, "The situation passes from Black to bleak."

Throwing a spitter, said Preacher Roe, is "like squeezing a watermelon seed between your fingers." The Preacher should know; he threw a lot of them. Umps warned him about his illegal habits, warnings that he generally disregarded. Walking up to ump Augie Donatelli one day, Roe said, "Augie, I ain't spoke to ya in two months, but I just want ya to know I still think you're horseshit."

Billy Loes, who once lost a ground ball in the sun, explained to a reporter why he never wanted to win twenty games in a season: "If you win twenty, they want you to do it every year."

Manager: The Dodgers had a few of them, but none like Charlie Dressen—or "Jolly Cholly," in Brooklynese. "Stay close," the ever-optimistic Dressen told his players. "I'll think of something."

If he did, you can bet it didn't come from a book. Cholly was a firm believer in the Rogers Hornsby axiom: "Don't read, it'll hurt your eyes." Asked why nobody ever saw him with a book in his hands, the fifty-four-year-old Dressen said, "I got this far without reading a book, I ain't gonna start now."

8
Big Apple vs. Big Orange

Unquestionably, in the eyes of Brooklyn fans, Walter O'Malley is the black hat of this piece, a devious, conniving Grinch who stole from them the best thing they ever had. It was he who forced out Branch Rickey in a power grab for ownership. The pressure he put on Red Barber, a Brooklyn institution, made Red quit. He criticized Jackie Robinson and tried to get him to knuckle under to his wishes. For him, Ebbets Field was too small, too old, too beat-up. In a key move O'Malley, said to be wary of the influx of blacks and Puerto Ricans into Brooklyn, convinced the kindly if gullible Giants owner, Horace Stoneham, to go along with his plan to move west, and the deal was done.

Bums, Peter Golenbock's excellent oral history of the Brooklyn franchise, reflects this ongoing antipathy towards O'Malley. At various points in the book Golenbock calls him a "ruthless, money-hungry scalawag"; "ambitious and conniving"; "the black widow waiting for its prey; a "Judas." Roger Kahn is quoted as saying that the Dodgers owner "planned and schemed all his life." Joe Flaherty, the late journalist, blames O'Malley for "the total destruction of a culture."

To anyone not directly involved, it may be hard to understand how people can generate such emotion some thirty years after the fact. The Los Angeles Dodgers are arguably the most successful franchise in baseball, drawing millions every year and fielding highly competitive teams. Dodger Stadium in Chavez Ravine is one of the best parks in the country. What gives?

The real gripe of the die-hard Brooklyn fans may, in fact, have nothing to do with Walter O'Malley per se. He may only be the object of larger frustrations and resentments.

In 1956, before the Dodgers and Giants strayed from the fold, New York City alone had three major league franchises. Baseball was essentially an Eastern affair. Only one city west of the Mississippi, Kansas City, had a big league club; it had moved there the year before from Philadelphia. Prior to that the westernmost outpost of the majors was St. Louis.

Contrast that to the situation today. New York has but two teams, while California has five (if you consider the San Francisco Giants part of the major leagues). Texas can claim

two franchises, and Seattle one. The country's demographics
have changed. Its population base, the sources of money
creation, the electoral college numbers have all shifted west-
ward, and baseball and the other pro sports have followed
this trend.

Beyond this, many New Yorkers—and, to be sure, people in other parts of the country—have a simmering resentment, if not contempt, for California. If you're going to steal
the Dodgers, take them to Toledo or Atlanta or Dubuque—
anywhere but LA! When the Steve Garvey–led Dodgers
played the Yankees in the World Series in the late seventies,
they were not simply a couple good ballclubs playing for all
the marbles, they represented a clash of worlds. The wimpy
Los Angelenos, said the New York media, were "too laid-
back," "too Hollywood," to survive in the hostile Yankee
Stadium environment. They couldn't hack it, they weren't
tough enough, and after the Dodgers caved in to the pressure, it confirmed their every expectation.

Conversely, after those Dodgers avenged their losses to
the Yankees and won it all in 1981, the year of the split
season, those in Los Angeles saw it as a vindication of *their*
lifestyle (California word). The lingering image of that Series must be that of the uptight Yankee owner, George
Steinbrenner, with a bandage on his broken hand after slugging a couple nonexistent hecklers in an elevator.

One beef that New Yorkers have against LA sports fans
is probably a fair one: They don't care as much. The mass
exodus from Dodger Stadium that occurs around the seventh inning of a game, even a close one, could never happen
in New York City. New York fans—indeed fans all over the
East, in Boston, Philly, Detroit—generally get more involved than their counterparts in the West. They don't just
applaud a good play and then sit back in their seats waiting
for the next piece of action. Up on the edge of their seats,
they're intensely aware of what's happening on the field,
caught up in a game the way Californians are only on special
occasions. It doesn't have to be a playoff or a pennant-
deciding series for New Yorkers to get stirred up about base-

ball. The game matters deeply to them. Why it matters so much—why it's so important—is much the same reason why old Brooklyn fans won't let go of their Dodgers.

9
Ebbets Field and
the Pastoral Longing

To read accounts of post-war Brooklyn by writers sympathetic to the Dodgers is to go back to a simpler, greener world that has now been lost.

The television was not omnipresent. In the hot weather people sat around on the stoops gabbing with their neighbors. Kids played ball on the streets. There were no pushers and thugs around, people went out at night without fear.

The neighborhoods were still strong. Brooklyn was broken into distinct ethnic areas—Italians, Irish, the Jews— where the people watched out for their own and took care of them. The streets were clean and not clogged with cars. In the afternoons or evenings, you tuned in Red Barber to get the game. In the morning, you picked up the paper to see the box scores or get the results of other games.

At the center of this small, bubbling universe was Ebbets Field. The fans at Wrigley or Fenway or any of the older downtown parks still standing can probably best appreciate what Ebbets meant to followers of the Dodgers. It was their home away from home—a green place, a safe spot. And it was, by all accounts, a wonderful place to watch a baseball game.

Red Barber said, "When you have a box seat at Brooklyn, you are practically playing the infield." According to one eyewitness, you were so close to the action on the field that you could see the cords in a player's neck tighten.

Roger Kahn writes, "Ebbets Field was a narrow cockpit, built of brick and iron and concrete, alongside a steep cobblestone slope of Bedford Avenue. Two tiers of grandstand pressed the playing area from three sides, and in thousands of seats fans could hear a ballplayer's chatter, notice details of a ballplayer's gait and, at a time when television had not yet assaulted illusion with the Zoomar lens, you could see, you could actually see, the actual expression on the actual face of an actual major leaguer as he played. *You could know what he was like!"*

The people of Brooklyn identified utterly with their Dodgers. More so than other cities with other teams? More so than Boston and the '75 Red Sox? More so than Milwaukee and the Brewers of Gorman Thomas and Robin Yount? Probably not. It's pure sentimental hogwash, nothing more, to maintain that the Brooklyn experience was unique and that fans today have missed out on something that is irretrievable.

That said, there are nevertheless substantial differences between the relationship of the Dodgers and their fans and modern ballclubs and theirs. For one, they were largely a homegrown team. Gil Hodges, Jackie Robinson, Duke Snider, Pee Wee Reese, Roy Campanella all came up through the Dodger farm system. They started with the club, and they stayed with the club. Fans watched them break in, grow and mature over a period of years.

Many of the Dodgers actually lived in Brooklyn. They did not own luxury condos in the Sun Belt; they lived year-round in the city where they played. Mr. and Mrs. Duke Snider and the Carl Erskines owned homes in the Bay Ridge section of Brooklyn. The Harold Reeses resided at 97th Street and Fort Hamilton Parkway. Jackie Robinson and his family lived in East Flatbush. These men were not just big league stars, they were neighbors.

Nor was the park out in the suburbs. It was in Brooklyn itself, in a neighborhood where families lived. Tiny old Ebbets Field was at the hub of an interlocking complex of friendships, associations, contacts, shared beliefs, assumptions and emotions. Traditionally looked down upon by the big-city hotshots from across the river, Brooklyners took immense pride in Ebbets Field—in that arena, at least, they were the equal of anybody from Manhattan or anywhere else.

By and large, Brooklyn fans were working class or working poor people and their sons and daughters. They didn't summer in the Hamptons; they didn't bop into Manhattan for an evening of theater. They went to the ball game. The Dodgers were their amusement and their passion.

What they found in the Dodgers was a dream-life unlike anything else in the rest of their lives. In his essay "My Baseball Years," Philip Roth talks about his infatuation with the game as a boy, saying that news of the two most cataclysmic events of his childhood—President Roosevelt's death and the destruction of Hiroshima—came to him when he was out playing ball.

"Chicago only began to exist for me as a real place, and to matter in American history," Roth writes, "when I became fearful (as a Dodger fan) of the bat of Phil Cavarretta, first baseman for the Chicago Cubs." He adds, "Baseball, as played in the big leagues, was something completely outside my own life that could nonetheless move me to ecstasy and tears; it could excite the imagination and hold the attention as much with minutiae as with high drama."

For Roth, and for other Dodger fans, baseball was a "long, hopeless love affair." But a love affair that vitalized their lives. With the Dodgers in town, Brooklyn fans were somebody. They were someplace. Brooklyn had an identity, and so did they.

There's an interesting footnote to the upheaval that took place after the Dodgers left Brooklyn. In most franchise shifts the cities change, but not the men. Fans in Oakland, say, still follow the football Raiders, now playing in Los Angeles, because they know the names and faces on the field so well.

That didn't happen in Brooklyn. That old gang really did break up after the Dodgers pulled out. Pee Wee Reese played a halfhearted season in LA, then retired. Campanella's disabling car crash occurred the winter prior to the team's debut in the West. Jackie Robinson quit rather than accept a trade. Duke Snider performed fairly well on the Coast, but his best years were behind him.

For the most part a new generation of Dodgers, with names like Koufax and Drysdale, were taking over, their ties to the East rapidly slipping away. The old order passed so quickly it was almost as if it hadn't existed at all. The fans left in Brooklyn looked across at their former team a continent away, and saw strangers.

10
Afterword

The cheering may have stopped, but die-hard Brooklyn fans have hung on to the memory of their team. And you have to hand it to them. By saying that some things are above profit, their continued loyalty to their lost Dodgers stands as a rebuke to any professional sports owner who would rip his team from its home surroundings in pursuit of more dollars.

A few years ago Pete Hamill, the writer, was sitting in a New York bar with a friend. As it developed, their conversation turned to the subject of evil in the modern world. On a lark they decided to each make a list of the three people they considered to be the most evil of all time. Each man made up his list separately, but both came up with the same three names. Their lists read:

1. Hitler
2. Stalin
3. Walter O'Malley

Brooklyn lives.

5

The Name Game: Some Ballplayers' Nicknames and How They Got Them

"Deep in the oldest traditions of the human race dwells the secret of the magical power of names . . ."

—JOHN COWPER POWYS, social historian

SMOKEY JOE

IT DOESN'T TAKE MUCH to get a nickname in baseball, and once you've got it you might as well forget about ever getting rid of it," said Joe Wood, who never got rid of his. A sportswriter, seeing the youngster pitch, said, "That kid sure throws smoke," and Smokey Joe had a nickname that stuck with him all his ballplaying days.

THE QUIET MAN

The longtime Quiet Man of the Dodgers, Walter Alston, apparently got his taciturn personality from his father. After watching his son's Brooklyn team win the World Series on TV, Alston Senior pulled out his shotgun, fired one shot in the air, and then sat down. When Walt returned home from his great triumph that year, his dad said, "Congratulations, but we have work to do." And the two men went out to do some chores on the family farm.

RAZOR SHINES

When this young prospect was playing in junior college, he was a terror at the plate, hitting balls so hard they seemed to slice up the air. About the only person who calls him Anthony now is his mother.

BIG ED

At six foot one, one hundred and ninety pounds, Big Ed Walsh was considered an exceptionally big man in the days before World War I. Since then our standards have gone up quite a bit. Nowadays people might call him "Average Ed."

MARVELOUS MARV

Marv Throneberry, formerly of the Mets, was called "Marvelous" because he was not. Given a birthday cake at a celebration in the Mets locker room, manager Casey Stengel said, "They'd a given one to Throneberry too, except they figured he'd probably drop it."

CY

While trying to impress an owner, Denton True Young tore some boards off a grandstand with his high-powered fastball. Somebody said that it looked like a cyclone had hit it. Cyclone was shortened to "Cy," and it's a good thing too. The "Denton True Young Award" for pitching excellence in the majors doesn't sound half as good.

FIRE TRUCKS

For a reliever, what better nickname than Virgil "Fire" Trucks?

BYE-BYE BALBONI

Home run hitters have some of the best nicknames. Steve "Bye-Bye" Balboni of the Royals has a good one, but there are others. A sampling: Ralph "Socks" Seybold, George "The Boomer" Scott, Larrupin' Lou Gehrig, Harmon "Killer" Killebrew and, of course, Frank "Home Run" Baker.

THE FLYING DUTCHMAN

The fabled Flying Dutchman operated under a misnomer; Honus Wagner's family actually came from

Germany, not Holland. But Ty Cobb knew the truth. Standing on first in a World Series game against the Pirates, Cobb yelled over at Wagner near second: "Get ready, Krauthead! I'm coming down!"

GRAIG NETTLES

Writes Art Hill, "Have you ever wondered how Graig Nettles got his unusual name? My theory is that his father wanted to name him Greg and his mother preferred Craig. So they compromised. Probably better than Creg, at that."

MR. BASEBALL

Johnny Carson now introduces Bob Uecker as "Mr. Baseball," but to baseball purists this is an abomination. For them there can be only one Mr. Baseball, and his name is Connie Mack.

BAD HENRY

Hank Aaron, because he was.

THE NIGHT RIDER

Between starts, Don "Night Rider" Larsen of the Yankees loved to ramble and romp in the late hours. Said a manager, "The only thing Larsen fears is sleep."

SHUFFLIN', SLIDIN', SCOOTER AND SWISH

Shufflin' Phil Douglas shuffled when he walked, Slidin' Bill Hamilton stole bases, and "Scooter" Rizzuto of the Yankees scooted after ground balls at shortstop.

But "Swish" Nicholson, late of the Cubs, did not himself swish—it was the sound the ball made as he watched it go past him for a third strike, which was often.

CHARLIE HUSTLE

In the minors they called Pete Rose "Hollywood," "José Hustle," and "Hotdog." The one that stuck, of course, was "Charlie Hustle." Pete and the new-ish owner of the Reds, Marge Schott, are known as "Hustle and Bustle."

TARZAN

The muscular Danny Gardella, an outfielder.

JUNIOR

To go along with all the "Kids" in baseball—Gary Carter, Ted Williams, Kid Elberfeld, etc.—there is "Junior" Gilliam, who began playing with the Baltimore Elite Giants of the National Negro League at the ripe old age of seventeen.

DOCTOR K

As a youngster Dwight Gooden was "Dr. D" or simply, "The Doctor," because he loved to watch Julius Erving ("Dr. J") play basketball and tried to copy his style.

Now with the Mets, he has become "Doctor K," strikeout artist supreme. Some also call him "The Heat Man."

PANCHO

Ex-Phillies utility man Pancho Herrera ought not to be confused with Pancho Segura, Pancho Gonzales and Sancho Panza, all of whom had nothing to do with baseball.

THE HAWK

First baseman Ken Harrelson, named for his prominent beak. Other major leaguers with distinctive body parts were

Footsie Marcum, Eddie "Knuckles" Cicotte, One Arm Dailey, Piano Legs Hickman and Clint Hartung, whose big ears earned him the nickname "Floppy."

MR. OCTOBER

Reggie Jackson got this designation after several years of outstanding post-season play, although his critics might say it's the only time of year he puts out. Also known as "Jax."

POPS & DADDY

Willie Stargell was "Pops" of "The Family," the raunchy and exuberant '79 World Champion Pirates.

Another father figure in baseball was Leon "Daddy Wags" Wagner, an outfield stalwart.

MOON MAN

Jay Johnstone, among others. The *Los Angeles Times* described Jay as "The Man Who Fell to Earth." An early seventies joke around the league when the flaky outfielder was playing for Chicago went like this:

Q: Where did the Sox get Johnstone?

A: Neil Armstrong brought him back.

FATTIES

Tubby I: Ernie Whitt, Blue Jays catcher.

Tubby II: Bill Caudill, Blue Jays pitcher.

Edward "Tubby" Spencer.

Fat Freddie Fitzsimmons.

Jumbo Jim Hearn.

Fat Bob, the Singing Plumber. Every season for the past umpteen years Fat Bob has opened Tiger Stadium with a rousing recital of "The Star-Spangled Banner."

Mickey Klutts: "The Man Who Ate Manhattan Beach." (Klutts grew up in Manhattan Beach.)

PUDGE

Not quite a fatty: Carlton Fisk, of the Sox.

BULLDOG

Hitters simply weren't going to be intimidated by a pitcher named Orel Hershiser. So the Dodgers made Orel "The Bulldog."

THE RABBI OF SWAT

A Jewish minor league slugger named Moses Solomon who appeared briefly in the majors.

STAN & DON

From Stan "The Man" Musial, who was known for his reliability, came Don "Stan the Man Unusual" Stanhouse, known for his *un*reliability.

THREE OF A KIND

Handy Andy Pafko could play almost any position, just as you could always count on pitcher Sheldon "Available" Jones to be ready if you needed him.

And in the unlikely event neither of these guys could perform for your team, give a call to Negro League player Ted "Double Duty" Radcliff, who could pitch and catch, but not at the same time.

SWEET LOU

As Phil Rizzuto has noted, the "Sweet" in Sweet Lou Piniella's nickname referred not to his personality, but his swing.

DOWNTOWN BROWN

Darrell "Downtown" Brown has hit only one homer in his career, which prompted his manager, Billy Gardner, to remark: "That must be an awful small town."

THE WIZARD OF OZ

Ozzie Smith. Who else?

BAREFOOT BOYS

Like Shoeless Joe Jackson, who played ball as a kid in his bare feet, Bobby Dews eschewed shoes when young, becoming known as "The Barefoot Catcher." Dews played his whole career in the minors. After finally getting a chance to coach in the big leagues, Dews was asked the difference between the majors and the minors. "The grass is greener, the sun's not as hot, and the dirt's not as dirty," he said.

THE MONSTER

Relief pitcher Dick Radatz, who was big and ugly and had a glare that made puppies yelp.

KONG (1)

A natural for Dave Kingman, the big home run hitter. Also: "Sky King."

KONG (2)

Charlie "King Kong" Keller, the Yankee slugger of the forties, was another who drew comparisons with the big ape. Said his teammate Lefty Gomez, "Keller is the first player to be brought back by Frank Buck."

Buck was a famous big game hunter of the time.

VIDA BLUE

When Vida Blue was starring for the A's, owner Charlie Finley asked him to change his name to "True." Finley thought a pitcher with the name of "True Blue" was a sure-fire ticket seller. Vida told him to shove it.

RAPID ROBERT

Rapid Robert Feller had a fastball that broke bats. Also known as Bullet Bob Feller, along with Bullet Joe Bush and Bullet Bob Gibson.

DOCK ELLIS

In the mid-seventies Dock Ellis was traded to the Yankees for Doc Medich, then a medical student. While Medich bombed on the Pirates, Ellis went on to win seventeen games that season. Said sportswriter Charles Feeney, "Ellis is probably a better doctor, too."

SCUZZ

"Scuzz" Grimsley, pitcher for the Orioles, had "enough greasy kid stuff in his ultra-long curly hair to give A. J. Foyt a lube job and an oil change," according to Tom Boswell.

THE IRON HORSE

Lou Gehrig, due to his amazing durability. The Yankee first baseman was also called "Biscuit Pants" by his teammates, though perhaps it would be indiscreet to inquire why.

GANCE MULLINORG

Garth Iorg and Rance Mulliniks of the Blue Jays. Because they platoon at third base, they are known, collectively, as "Gance Mullinorg."

FOREIGN AND DOMESTIC

Of all the regions of the country, the South produces the most colorful names. Georgia-born Ty Cobb was "The Georgia Peach," Enos "Country" Slaughter grew up on a North Carolina tobacco farm, and native son Ron Guidry is "Louisiana Lightnin'." Kenesaw Mountain Landis, the first commissioner of baseball, was named after one of the bloodiest battles of the Civil War, the Battle of Kennesaw Mountain in Georgia.

Spanning the globe for other nationalities, we find Irish Meusel, Swede Risberg (one of the Black Sox), Frenchy Bordagaray, Germany Schaefer, Dutch Leonard (one of many Dutches to be involved in the game, including "Dutch" Reagan, former Cubs broadcaster and president of the United States), "Turk" Farrell, Juan Marichal ("The Dominican Dandy"), and Al "The Little Italian" Gionfriddo.

PEE WEE

Dodger shortstop Harold Reese was a little guy, but that's not how he came to be known as "Pee Wee." Young Harold played marbles, winning the Kentucky state championship at thirteen with his deadly accurate use of the Pee Wee marble.

MIGHTY MOUSE

Another little guy, Solly Hemus, infielder for the Cards.

WEE WILLIE

An even littler little guy, Wee Willie Keeler, who used to hit 'em where they weren't.

A LOTTA BULL

Orlando Cepeda, the hard-hitting first baseman, was "The Baby Bull." Which makes sense. His father, a great slugging star in his own right in the Puerto Rican leagues, was known as "The Bull."

CHAMP SUMMERS

John J. Summers, utility man. His father, an ex-Navy boxer, gave him his nickname. Explains Champ: "I was so ugly that when my father first saw me, he thought I had already gone ten rounds with Joe Louis."

BUCKETFOOT

Like Master Mel Ott, Al "Bucketfoot" Simmons had a peculiar hitting stance but got Hall of Fame production from it.

ACADEMICS

Player-manager Frankie Frisch, "The Fordham Flash," starred in the big three sports in college.

Columbia George Smith, a pitcher, went to—surprise!—Columbia University.

Joe DiMaggio's brother Dominic, "The Little Professor," looked like he belonged in class, not on a ball field.

Another bespectacled ballplayer, Jim "The Professor" Brosnan, wrote *The Long Season,* one of the better inside accounts of a major leaguer's life.

SCHOOLBOY, THE MERRY MORTICIAN

Waite "Schoolboy" Hoyt made the majors while only a teenager, and later starred for the Yankees.

They also called the hang-loose pitcher "The Merry Mortician." His dad was an undertaker, and Waite worked the business in his spare time. One day he got a call to pick up a corpse near Yankee Stadium. No problem, said Waite, who picked up the body and left it in the trunk of his car while he stopped off to pitch a shutout for the Yankees. After the game he delivered it to its appointed destination.

THE HIT MAN

Mike Easler, a member of Boston's 1985 "Hit Squad," a power lineup feared around the American League.

SILK

Silk O'Loughlin, the old-time umpire, was smooth and oh so slick. He kept his pants so perfectly pressed that "players were afraid to slide when Silk was close for fear they'd bump against the trousers and cut themselves," said Christy Mathewson.

MOOSES

Not only was Walt "Moose" Dropo as big as a moose, he came from Moosup, Connecticut.

As the Cardinals hammered Brewers pitcher Moose Haas in a World Series game, Vin Scully commented, "They're about to stuff the Moose and hang him on the wall."

Moose Skowron of the Yankees had his rough moments

too, slumping badly one season. Said his manager Casey Stengel, "The way he's going, I'd be better off if he was hurt."

THE RAJAH

The marvelous batsman Rogers Hornsby. Toward the end of his life, well after he had retired, Hornsby participated in an old-timer's game and struck out in his only appearance. Lefty Gomez said, "After twenty-five years we finally learned how to pitch to him."

PURPLE HAYES

Thanks to Chris Berman, the broadcaster, we now have Von "Purple" Hayes. Other choice Bermanisms: Bruce "Eggs" Benedict, Frank Tanana Daiquiri, Dan "Man From" Gladden, Julio "Won't You Take Me on a Sea" Cruz, Jim "Hound Dog" Presley.

LEO THE LIP

Silent Mike Tiernan would not have gotten a word in edgewise if he'd ever played under The Lip. "To have a long talk with me all you have to do is say hello," said Durocher, who was also labeled "Fifth Avenue," for the flashy, expensive duds he wore.

Two major leaguers who probably could've held their own in a conversation with The Lip were Paul "Motormouth" Blair and Charles "Gabby" Hartnett.

GRANDMA

The two theories as to how Johnny Murphy got saddled with this one:

1) He bitched like an old lady on road trips.
2) He pitched with a creaky rocking-chair motion.

MR. WARMTH

Ex-Brewers left-hander Mike Caldwell, for his lack of same.

BUGS

A pitcher in the early 1900s, Arthur "Bugs" Raymond was buggy. Asked one year what he planned to do in the off-season, Bugs said, "I am in doubt. I may either run a locomotive for the Great Northern Railroad or become a newspaperman."

THE FLEA

Miller Huggins, the tiny Yankee manager. Once, so the story goes, Babe Ruth hung Huggins out the back of a moving train by his heels.

THE POISONS

Lloyd Waner: Little Poison. His brother Paul: Big Poison. A pitcher needed black tea and burnt toast after facing these two great Pirate hitters.

RAGS

Locker-room short for Righetti. A few seasons back, with Ron Guidry hurting, Dave was about all the Yankees had in the way of pitching. A sportswriter summed up the team's staff as "Righetti and meatballs."

WAHOO SAM

Wahoo Sam Crawford was not a wahoo; rather he came from Wahoo, Nebraska, and loved to be associated with his hometown.

THE CATS AND THE HAT

Harvey "Kitten" Haddix pitched a lot like Harry "The Cat" Brecheen, who teamed on the Cardinals with outfielder Harry "The Hat" Walker. Always nervously tugging on his cap, The Hat wore out an average of two or three dozen caps a year.

YOGI

Lawrence Peter Berra may have first been called "Yogi" by his boyhood chums back in St. Louis; it was their term for oddball.

Or: Some teammates may have coined the expression after seeing Yogi sitting with his legs crossed in the style of a Hindu fakir.

Whatever the derivation, Yogi most definitely did *not* get his nickname from Yogi Bear, the cartoon character that appeared after the Yankee catcher came into prominence.

BAMBI

George Bamberger is Bambi, like the deer. When he managed the hard-hitting Milwaukee Brewers of a few years ago, they were known as "Bambi's Bombers." Under Harvey Kuenn the Brewers were "Harvey's Wallbangers."

WHITEY HERZOG

Of all the Whiteys to populate the game of baseball, this one may be the most grateful. Who would not want a nickname—*any* nickname—with a first name like Dorrel?

They also call Herzog "The White Rat" because, some say, he looks like one.

SPANKY AND OUR GANG

Ex-Royal Ed Kirkpatrick was a squat, slow-footed catcher with a potbelly—hence, "Spanky." If you put Ed together with Hall of Famer Zack Wheat, you'd have Spanky and Buck Wheat. Then all you'd need would be Alfalfa . . .

THE GREAT ONE

Roberto Clemente. Need we say more?

FLASH

An obvious but still slick name for a sure-fielding second baseman: Joe "Flash" Gordon.

WONDER BATS

Roy Hobbs, power-hitting outfielder for the New York Knights, called his bat "Wonderboy." Cut from a tree that had been split open by lightning, Wonderboy did indeed perform wondrous feats. Journeyman Jay Johnstone deemed his bat "My Business Partner" and Al Bumbry, formerly of the Orioles, dubbed his "The Soul Pole." The hottest lickin' stick of all may have been Joe Jackson's black bat, appropriately known as "Black Beauty." Reasoning that bats, like people, appreciate the warm weather, Jackson took all his bats with him south for the winter.

PEP YOUNGS

A forerunner of Pete Rose. This New York Giants outfielder was known for his peppy, boyish enthusiasm.

THE BABE, ETC.

George Herman Ruth was a nickname factory all by himself. Though now gone out of favor, "Babe" was a popular boys' nickname in the early part of the century; it implied a baby-faced kid, an innocent. Sportswriters called Ruth "Dunn's Baby," after the owner-manager of his first pro team. He quickly grew up to become "The Home Run King," "The Sultan of Swat," and "The Mightiest Slugger of Them All." "The Mauler" described the way he attacked baseballs. "Bambino" was the Italian word for Babe. He answered to "Jidge," a bastardization of George. Mexican newspapers proclaimed him "El Rey Jonronero." Ruth and Gehrig were "The Home Run Twins" or "Five O'Clock Lightning," so named for their ability to come through with thunderclap home runs in the late innings of an afternoon game. Yankee Stadium is The House That Ruth Built. Ruth was the bulwark of the original Murderer's Row, and as he got older the men who came in to replace him late in a game were known as "Ruth's caddies."

But! The inspiration for the candy bar came not from the Yankee slugger, but from Baby Ruth, the girl born to President and Mrs. Grover Cleveland during his term of office.

ODDIBE McDOWELL

With a name like Oddibe, Oddibe ought to be a star.

GRAPEFRUIT

The portly manager Wilbert Robinson, who looked like one.

MILITARY MEN

Sarge: Gary Matthews of the Cubs, a take-charge guy if there ever was one.

The Li'l Colonel: Pee Wee Reese, Kentucky-born field commander of the Brooklyn Dodgers.

The Little General: Gene Mauch.

The General: Alvin Crowder. During World War I General Enoch Crowder—no relation—supervised the draft and the conscription of ballplayers. He became so familiar to players that when Alvin, a pitcher, entered the big leagues in the late twenties, he was instantly nicknamed "General" Crowder.

WEAPONRY

The Toy Cannon: Jimmy Wynn, an outfielder who packed a wallop despite his small size.

The Reading Rifle: Carl Furillo, who shot down baserunners from right field.

Shotgun George Shuba, outfielder.

Pistol Pete Reiser.

LUCKY LOHRKE

Jack Lohrke failed to show for a bus that crashed, and later just missed taking a plane that went down in flames. Is it any wonder people called the New York Giants infielder "Lucky"?

DR. STRANGEGLOVE OR STONEFINGERS

By any of his names, Dick Stuart was a terrible-fielding first baseman. At a game in Pittsburgh the P.A. announcer made his customary pregame warning, "Anyone interfering with a ball in play will be ejected from the ballpark," etc. To which Danny Murtaugh, Dick's manager, said, "God, I hope Stuart doesn't think that means him."

EYE CHART

Doug Gwosdz (pronounced "Goosh"), the catcher, whose name could pass for the last line of a doctor's eye chart.

DANNY CARTER

Danny Cater's teammates called him "Carter" because his name was so often spelled that way in the box scores.

BULL DURHAM

With his name, Leon should be a spokesman for the tobacco industry.

D DAY

D Day was, in Brooklynese, Dat Day, the game Bobby Thomson of the Giants hit The Shot Heard 'Round The World that beat the Brooklyn Dodgers in the '51 playoffs.

THE BARBER

Sal Maglie, of course. For his willingness—nay, eagerness—to shave hitters with fastballs close to their whiskers.

GOOFY

Lefty Gomez was also "Goofy" Gomez, a flake of legendary proportions and a fine comic storyteller (not to mention a Hall of Fame pitcher).

Here's one from Lefty: In the '32 Series, Cubs righthander Lon Warneke ("The Arkansas Hummingbird") refused to pose for a photograph with Gomez, who was pitching against him. "What's a matter, Lon?" Lefty asked him. "You superstitious?" Warneke replied, "Superstitious, hell. I just think it's unlucky."

TOM TERRIFIC

The upstanding role model of the Miracle Mets, Tom Seaver.

MAD DOG, THE MAD HUNGARIAN

With his fearsome mien and Fu Manchu mustache, Al Hrabosky came out of the bullpen snorting like a rabid dog. Said Mad Al: "Hitters are my archenemies. I hate 'em. I approach them as if they just said something nasty about my mother."

THE MAD MONK

A cousin, in baseball genealogy, to Mad Dog Hrabosky was short-tempered pitcher Russ Meyer—"The Mad Monk" or "Russell the Redneck Reindeer."

THE TINKLE TWINS

Don Mattingly and Dale Berra, teammates on the Yankees, were both arrested and fined for relieving themselves in a public place during the 1985 season. The *New York Post* promptly dubbed them "The Tinkle Twins."

CASEY AND SATCH

The stories abound on how two legends of baseball, Charles Dillon Stengel and Leroy Robert Paige, arrived at their nicknames.

Casey: Some say it came from the poem "Casey at the Bat" and Stengel's alleged penchant for striking out in the clutch. Others claim that his signature used to be "K.C.

Stengel," in honor of his hometown of Kansas City, Missouri. People called him "K.C." and Stengel liked it so much he changed the spelling and took on the name.

Satchel: Denying he got his name from "Satchelfoot," a crude reference to his size fourteen shoes, Paige claimed he picked up the moniker when he was a young man porting luggage at the railroad station in Mobile, Alabama, where he grew up.

THE BIG DONKEY

Outfielder Frank Thomas. Though Frank's bat had some kick in it, explains Bob Uecker, he was always putting his big foot in his mouth.

DUCKY AND THE PENGUIN

"Ducky" Medwick of the Gashouse Gang waddled like a duck, much like a contemporary ballplayer, Ron "The Penguin" Cey.

DAZZY

Hall of Fame right-hander Dazzy Vance dazzled hitters with a potent array of pitches. His curve, remembered Rube Bressler, was "like an apple rolling off a crooked table."

After being struck out by Vance on a fastball, Jigger Statz said, "I couldn't see it, but it sounded low."

TIP

Tip O'Neill was an accomplished scratch hitter who specialized in fouling off ball after ball until the pitcher got tired and walked him. Many Irish-American families at the turn of the century idolized him, and named their sons after him. One prominent example: Speaker of the House Thomas P. "Tip" O'Neill.

RUBE

Richard William Marquard became "Rube" after someone noticed his strong facial resemblance to another great left-hander of the time, Rube Waddell. Waddell, by the way, was dubbed "The Sousepaw" for all his drinking.

COMET TALES

Most everyone knows that Mickey Mantle was "The Commerce Comet," but who can name "The Hoosier Comet?"

Answer: Indiana's Oscar Charleston, speedy center fielder in the old Negro Leagues.

MORE MICKEYS

Muff Mantle, Mickey's coal-mining father, named his son after his favorite ballplayer, Mickey Cochrane, whose real name was Gordon Stanley Cochrane. An early manager thought young Gordon looked Irish and started calling him "Mickey." To confuse things still more, Newton Grasso, primarily known as Mickey Grasso, got *his* nickname because he looked so much like Cochrane.

JOHNNIE DISASTER

When Johnnie LeMaster entered the majors, they declared shortstop a disaster area.

KID NATURAL & FRIENDS

Keith Moreland, who's known as "Zonk," after the *Doonesbury* cartoon character, calls Ryne Sandberg "Kid Natural," which is far more poetic than another name the second baseman goes by: "Ryno." Their teammmate on the Cubs is Bob Dernier, "The Deer," a speedy outfielder. Dernier and Sandberg were on base together so much one season that Harry Caray labeled them "The Daily Double."

THE TERMINATOR

Expos reliever Jeff Reardon, who snuffs out rallies.

SEÑOR SMOKE

Fernando Valenzuela, the Mexican-born ace of the Dodger pitching staff. Aurelio Lopez, Detroit's fastball-throwing relief pitcher, is also sometimes called Señor Smoke.

LE GRAND ORANGE

What the French-speaking fans of Montreal used to call Rusty Staub, the ageless redheaded pinch-hitting wonder.

EDDIE MATTRESS

Eddie Mathews, Braves third baseman. The good German burghers of Milwaukee couldn't pronounce their hero's name properly, so they yelled, "Get a hit, Eddie Mattress! Get a hit!"

THE LONE WOLF

In Japanese, *ippiki okami* means "Lone Wolf," the name given to Yukata Enatsu, a maverick pitcher in the Japanese leagues who tried unsuccessfully to cut it in American ball in a recent tryout with the Brewers.

THREE FINGER BROWN

Born in 1876, Mordecai Peter Centennial Brown became Three Finger Brown after he lost the tip of the index finger of his pitching hand and part of his little finger in an accident.

THE VULTURE

Phil "The Vulture" Regan swooped in for late-inning saves.

THE HUMAN CRAB

Second baseman Johnny Evers, who suffered a nervous breakdown, was a very, very intense individual who was difficult to be around. Players around the league referred to him as "The Human Crab."

ALL ABOARD!

Trains are a favorite motif in baseball nicknames. Walter "Big Train" Johnson had a locomotive-driven fastball. Joe DiMaggio was named after a speedy Boston–New York commuter train (and a great sailing ship), The Yankee Clipper. Tommy Henrich, DiMaggio's Yankee teammate, was known as "Ol' Reliable," another train. Then there was Clarence "Choo Choo" Coleman, catcher for the Mets.

SLATS, STRETCH, STEEPLE AND STICK

"Slats" was the long-legged Connie Mack (aka "The Tall Tactician"). "Stick" is Gene Michael of the Yankees, equally tall and thin. "Stretch," among many others, can be claimed by Willie McCovey, the lean and powerful Giants first baseman. And "Steeple" was Howie Schultz, a towering first baseman with deep religious feelings.

NUFF CED

The Royal Rooters were a fanatical group of Boston baseball fans in the late 1800s. Their leader was Mike "Nuff Ced" McGreevey, who ran the bar in which they all congregated. In the evenings after work the Rooters would get into uproariously loud arguments over their favorite subject. When McGreevey grew tired of their discussion, or if it had gotten out of hand, he would put an end to it by yelling at the top of his voice, "Enough said!"

6

It's Cocktail Time! Topics, Oft of an Indelicate Nature, That You Can Toss Around at a Party or in a Bar

"Baseball is just an opinion."

—CHUCK TANNER, baseball manager

Baseball and the Bottle

WHEN YANKEES Don Mattingly and Dale Berra were caught peeing in public outside a Kansas City restaurant during the 1985 season, they were continuing a baseball tradition of drunkenness and rowdy public behavior that is as old as the game itself. Baseball players have never been saints. They used to drink before games, after games, *during* games. They came to the games drunk, and the fresh air and exercise helped sober them up.

Before the turn of the century Mike "King" Kelly was a superstar with an outrageously big salary—"It will be remembered that for his salary, Mr. Kelly works but a few months in the summer season," carped a reporter circa 1891—who helped pioneer a daring new baserunning technique called the slide. And did Mr. Kelly drink during your typical baseball game? "It depends on the length of the game," he said. In 1903 a Cincinnati newspaper published this advice to the hometown Redlegs, a team widely known for its alcoholic indulgences:

"Whenever a ball looks like this:

O

O

O

Take a chance on the middle one."

Of the men who played the game in the early decades of the twentieth century, baseball historian Lawrence Ritter wrote, "They were pioneers, in every sense of the word, engaged in a pursuit in which only the most skilled, the most determined, and above all, the most rugged, survived. They entered an endeavor which lacked social respectability, and when they left it, it was America's National Game." For these old-timers drinking was not an aberration; it was part of their lives as ballplayers, part of the rambunctious, free-wheeling, barnstorming life of men who at times would not be seated in a hotel dining room because they, and their trade, were not respectable enough.

Though baseball became socially acceptable, the habits of the players themselves did not change much over the years. They were as rowdy and intemperate as ever. Of slugger Hack Wilson, a writer said, "Gin was his tonic." Babe Ruth and Waite Hoyt ran around together on the Yankees in the twenties, drinking and carousing till all hours of the night. But the pace got to be too much for Hoyt, who checked into a hospital to dry out. When the newspapers, according to the *Baseball Digest*'s John Kuenster, reported Hoyt's problem as "amnesia," Ruth sent him a telegram in the hospital: "Read about your case of Amnesia. Must be a new brand."

Stories like these are rife, a part of the enduring lore of the game. In spring training the year after his perfect game in the World Series, Don Larsen wrapped his car around a phone pole at five in the morning after a night of boozy adventuring. Asked about the incident, his manager Casey Stengel winked and said, "Gee, that's kinda late to go out to mail a letter, ain't it?"

Stengel had a phrase for ballplayers who drank a lot: "whiskey slick." One whiskey-slick Yankee was Joe Page, a relief pitcher. "If Joe Page is seen in a liquor store at nine o'clock at night," said one wag, "the next morning it's ninety-nine proof."

In a more contemporary vein, an Angel star said at the end of his career, "If I ever decide to do a book I've already got the title: *The Bases Were Loaded and So Was I.*" Watching reformed alcoholic Bob Welch throw a one-hitter for the Dodgers, broadcaster Skip Caray said, "You see somebody pitch like this, it's enough to make you want to go on the wagon."

Yet for all their good-natured jocularity, these drinking tales often contain notes of sadness or even cruelty. Leo Durocher wrote of Horace Stoneham, former owner of the Giants: "There are two things that make it difficult to work for Stoneham when he's drinking: 1) Sometimes you can find him. 2) Sometimes you can't." It's been pointed out by many that Billy Martin's public fights invariably occur when he's been drinking. And when the hard-throwing right-hander Ryne Duren, also a reformed alcoholic, says, "I never really knew what it was like to pitch a sober inning," you have to wonder. Here was a guy pitching in the major leagues, doing what a lot of boys and men would trade a fortune to do, and for whatever reason he couldn't take it on its own terms and simply enjoy it.

If there's anything new about what's going on today, it's that the boys of baseball, while still relishing a taste for the Devil's Elixir, have graduated to drugs. Bill Conlin writes, "Drinking has long been the pastime of men in the National Pastime, but it will take a hundred years of cocaine and marijuana use to come close to matching the lives and careers shattered by abuse of beverages that are available in every major league clubhouse and the harder stuff that is imbibed in every hotel bar and watering hole that caters to jocks."

ADDENDUM

Talk about drugs puts one in mind of an old story that circulated around the majors in the early seventies. A baseball manager was having a clubhouse talk with his players, some of whom were suspected of smoking marijuana. Reminding them of the dangers of the drug, he warned that anyone violating the club's strict rules against pot use would be treated severely, and sent immediately down to the minor leagues.

"Boys," he said sternly. "All I have to say is that if one of you gets caught with Mary Jane, you better be hitting four-fucking-eighty at the All-Star break!"

The Longest Hit That Ever Was

Babe Ruth hit a lot of long home run balls, the longest of the long being an approximately six hundred foot shot in a 1919 spring training game. "I believe it was the longest hit I ever saw," said Giants manager John McGraw, who saw his share of big home runs in his time. But McGraw was not on hand when an obscure minor leaguer named "Dizzy" Carlyle supposedly hit a baseball, in 1929, that traveled six hundred eighteen feet in the air, what some claim is the farthest ever. After that Bunyanesque stroke Carlyle returned to anonymity, leaving the argument of who hit the longest home run of all time to be waged by generations to come in perpetuity.

The reason why everybody gets so worked up about this subject is that memory, not science, provides the yardstick for measuring these homers, and as the person who witnessed the clout gets older, his recollection of how far the ball traveled keeps getting longer and longer. Funny how that works.

Josh Gibson, the prodigious Negro League slugger, reportedly hit a ball out of Yankee Stadium, the only man to do so. Those who played with Gibson swore his power surpassed that of Ruth or Gehrig or anybody. Said James "Cool Papa" Bell, "Ruth used to hit them high. Not Gibson. He hit them *straight.*"

A contemporary of Gibson's in the white leagues was Jimmie Foxx, who was known as "The Beast" for his animal-like strength and peaceful good nature. His muscles, according to an old story, could hold thirty-five pounds of air. Players in the American League would point out to visitors the faraway spots in their ballparks where a Foxx blast had landed. After The Beast hit a soaring home run in Yankee Stadium, Lefty Gomez said, "I don't know how far it went, but I do know it takes forty-five minutes to walk up there." Again: Foxx pasted a ball in a World Series that never seemed to come down. A bullpen wit who saw it said, "We watched it fly for two innings."

It was not really until Mickey Mantle came along that an attempt was made to measure accurately these long home runs. Yankee front-office people would scurry around the outer reaches of ballparks calculating the distance of his best shots with a tape measure; thus, the origin of "the tape-measure home run." The switch-hitting Mantle almost hit a ball out of Yankee Stadium himself (left-handed), but his longest came in D.C. against the Senators. He hit it right-handed and it went five hundred sixty-five feet. But what was so remarkable about Mantle, say his old pal Billy Martin and others, was that he hit those sorts of rockets all the time. For Mantle, a four hundred fifty–footer was another day at the office.

While the Mick gets high marks for consistency, many would nevertheless challenge—to the death!—the assertion that the top ranking belongs to him. His teammate Roger Maris, said Casey Stengel, "had more power than Stalin," and hit a lot a long way before, during and after the year he broke Ruth's record. Frank Howard, a giant of a Dodger, hit a big home run in the '63 World Series that landed some four hundred forty feet from home plate—the first fair ball to reach the second deck at Dodger Stadium.

And what would a discussion of this sort be without figuring in the contributions of one Willie Howard Mays? One Mays surface-to-air missile at the Polo Grounds left everyone who saw it in ruins. "I never saw a ball get out of a fuckin' ballpark so fuckin' fast in my entire fuckin' life," recalled the eloquent Leo Durocher, who was managing Mays at the time. "He swings and bang, it's clearing the fuckin' roof and it's still going up." Later on Mays hit another equally astounding homer off Warren Spahn, who said of his delivery, "For the first sixty feet it was a helluva pitch." And Mays's teammate on the Giants, big Willie Mc-Covey, called "the most awesome hitter I've ever seen" by Gene Mauch, used to hit balls out of windblown Candlestick Park into the parking lot.

Of today's whackers, certainly no one need feel embarrassed about how they fare in this department. Jim Rice, Gary Carter, George Foster, Mike Schmidt, Dale Murphy—these are all "big, hairy-assed bastards" (to use a favorite Charlie Dressen phrase) who can crush the ball. But you don't have to be a superstar to launch one; all it takes is for the pitcher to groove one and the man at the plate to be on his stroke. Said broadcaster Ken Coleman after watching a Bob Watson homer sail out of sight, "They usually show movies on a flight like that." Cincy's Eric Davis, in his first season in the big leagues, hit two massive opposite field shots at Riverfront Stadium, one against the upper-deck facade in right field. Observing this convincing display of raw power, the Reds manager called the young star over to his side. "Don't you listen to anybody but me," Pete Rose told Davis, "and you'll make a lot of money in this game."

Two more names, those of Kingman and Jackson, must not be left out. They are men who, to borrow a phrase from Casey Stengel, can "hit a ball over a building and through

the wind." "When Dave Kingman is connecting," ex-teammate Ed Kranepool said, "the only way to defense him is to
sit in the upper deck." After one royal Kingman blast Kranepool said admiringly that he could have chopped it into
thirty-five singles.

As for Reggie Jackson, some of the most admiring comments about his home run power have come (predictably)
from Reggie himself. After one Fenway Park blast, he said,
"It was an insurance homer. That's why I hit it halfway to
the Prudential Building." And: "I hit that ball so far my eyes
weren't good enough to see it land. That one had some
voltage."

Describing how it feels to connect, *really* connect, with a
pitch, Reggie told the *Los Angeles Times:* "Every once in a
while, if I really hit one, four hundred fifty feet or more, I'll
say to myself, 'Damn, that son of a gun's *hit*.' I've hit balls
that've wowed myself. 'Wow! I hit *that*?'" A Jackson long
shot that wowed everyone privileged enough to see it came
during the 1971 All-Star Game. Earlier in the game Johnny
Bench hit a home run ball high in to the upper deck at Tiger
Stadium, some fifty feet above the 415-foot mark in right
center, but that was nothing compared to Reggie's. It took
off on a direct, rising line that most certainly would have
cleared the roof if it hadn't hit the right field light tower. Al
Kaline, the Tiger Hall of Famer, said it was the hardest ball
he'd ever seen hit at Tiger Stadium or anywhere else. "I'm
only sorry it hit something," he said, speaking for all.

The capacity crowd was buzzing for minutes afterward,
and if it wasn't the longest ball ever hit in history, it probably
was the longest home run ever witnessed by a nationwide
television audience. Red Smith wrote, "It was taking off for
Windsor, Ontario, when it smashed against the light tower
on the right field roof, approximately ten stories high. Starting with Ted Williams in 1939, only eight players have hit
fair balls out of this park. Except for the light standard,
Reggie would be the first to hit one out of the country."

Chatter, Chatter
All Around the Diamond

1
On the Mound

What they talk about when they talk on the mound remains ever a source of mystery and speculation among fans. There are no microphones out there, no reporters scribbling notes—just a pitcher, catcher, the manager, and an infielder or two. Whatever do they say?

Bob Gibson, coaching with the Braves, went out to speak to a pitcher who was getting shellacked. The pitcher promptly settled down and got through the inning without suffering any more damage, and in the locker room afterward someone asked the former Cardinal great what advice he had given the young man. Gibson said, "I just told him if there weren't fifteen thousand people watching, I'd hit him in the head."

Other managers and coaches are just as abrupt with their charges. In winter league one year Tommy Lasorda came out to yank the frustrated Pedro Borbon, who threw the ball into the stands. "Damn," said Lasorda, "that's the hardest I've seen you throw all day."

In a World Series Lasorda trudged out to the mound to rescue Doug Rau, who was proving no mystery to Yankee bats. "You can't take me out," the left-hander complained, "there's a left-handed hitter up next." Lasorda, rigged up with a portable mike for a television special, was furious at his pitcher, saying (expletives deleted): "Listen. I am the manager of this team and I can take you out any time I want. So give me the ball now! And if you think you're so hot with left-handers, how come those three guys on the bases are left-handers, huh?"

Since microphones do not ordinarily accompany managers on their visits to the pitcher, the best mound stories venture very quickly into the realm of the apocryphal. The most famous of these involves Yankee stars Bill Dickey and Lefty Gomez, in a huddle discussing what to throw the man at bat, the dangerous Jimmie Foxx. Dickey had flashed the signs for a fastball, a curve and a change-up—and his pitcher had shook them all off.

"You tell me," Dickey demanded. "What do you want to throw him?"

"To tell you the truth, I don't want to throw the ball at all," replied Lefty.

Another twosome who had trouble with the signs were Roy Campanella and Don Newcombe of the Brooklyn Dodgers. "Newk," Campy told his pitcher, who was getting hit around the lot, "you better do somethin', 'cause when I signal for the Express you're throwin' me the Local."

Some years ago Walter Rabb, a university baseball coach, demanded the ball from his young pitcher. "Please, coach," begged the pitcher, "let me face this guy. I know I can get him. Last time he was up I struck him out." Rabb looked over at the batter and said, "That's true, son. But if you'll just think back, the last time he was up was in this same inning."

Jim Kern, relieving for the Rangers, bridled when his manager told him he had to come out of the game. "I'm not tired," Kern protested. "No, but your outfielders sure are," said the manager.

As you might expect, there are some farfetched Casey Stengel stories in this mode. In one a young pitcher gives up a very long home run, explaining that it came off his best pitch, a curveball. "Lissen," says a sad-faced Casey. "If it breaks over the plate, it ain't a curve." Another has Casey managing the Mets and going out to the mound after a fly landed on his pitcher's nose, causing him to balk. Casey's advice: "Young man, if you want to pitch in the majors, you'll have to learn to catch those in your mouth."

According to Jim Bouton, Seattle manager Joe Schultz used to walk out to the mound, pick up the resin bag and throw it down, and then tell his pitchers, "What the shit. Give 'em some low smoke and we'll catch an early plane the hell outta here."

Schultz's advice was a lot like Ed Ott's, when Ed was catching Kent Tekulve on the Pirates. "Say we're playing in Philadelphia," Ott explained to *Sports Illustrated*. "I just want to give both of us a breather. So I just stroll out there and we assume this confidential crisis position, our heads together. And I say, 'Listen, dummy, I hate to rush you on a lovely summer evening like this, but I've got a table reserved at Bookbinders in about half an hour and I'm hungry.' Then I'll stroll on back, looking serious for all the fans, and Teke will strike out whoever is left."

2
Around the Plate

The dialogue in the batter's box—between hitter and catcher, hitter and ump, catcher and ump, or all of them screaming simultaneously at one another—is no less colorful than that which takes place on the mound. The best stuff involves the men in blue and is told in Chapter Nine (see "Ump Humor"), but one story can be related in this space to give a flavor of these exchanges. Masanori Murakami, the only Japanese-born citizen to play in the major leagues, pitched two years for the Giants in the early sixties before packing it up and going home. He spoke very little English and, as Bob Uecker has pointed out, his favorite American songs were "Horro, Dorry" and "Up a Razy Liver." Since Murakami had such trouble with the language, a couple of his teammates took him aside to give him instructions on how to greet the umpire, Chris Pelekoudas. Committing the words to memory after practicing them over and over again, Murakami approached the ump before a game, bowed, and said, "Herro, you haily plick. How you like to piss up a lope?"

The catcher initiates most of the chatter around the plate

to break up the hitter's concentration. Gary Carter of the Mets is a big talker. So was Roy Campanella. "From the start catching appealed to me as a chance to be in the thick of the game continuously," Campy has written. "I never had to be lonely behind the plate where I could talk to the hitters. I also learned that by engaging them in conversation I could sometimes distract them."

One classic attempt at distraction came during a World Series between the Yankees and the Braves, with Bad Henry Aaron at the plate. "Henry," said Yogi Berra, the Yankees catcher, "you don't want to break your bat. Better turn it around so you can read the trademark." Bad Henry glowered, "Yogi, I didn't come up here to read."

A half-century ago in an All-Star game, the weak-hitting pitcher Lefty Gomez got set in the batter's box, ready to take his cuts against the incomparable Giant screwballer, Carl Hubbell. The catcher, Gabby Hartnett, said to Gomez, "Are you trying to insult Hubbell—coming up here with a bat?"

Joe Garagiola, the catcher cum broadcaster, also liked to razz the opposition, which comes as no surprise to anyone who's heard his patter on NBC's *Game of the Week*. Joe had his best years as a player with St. Louis before being shuffled over to some other teams, where he had the chance to get the goat of his old Cardinal teammate, the indefatigable Stan Musial. Only it didn't work; Musial's goat was not to be had. As Garagiola tells it, "I'm a sociable guy, and I greeted all the players as they came to the plate so they wouldn't concentrate too much on their batting. It was always the same with Stan. I'd say, 'Hi, Stan, how's your family?' and as he crossed home plate a few seconds later he'd always answer, 'Fine, Joe, how's your family?'"

3
In the Pen

The strangest things on a ball field probably happen in the bullpen, out there removed from the action and sometimes out of sight of most of the spectators. Tug McGraw, who saved games for pennant winners in New York and Philadelphia, was typical of the bullpen breed. Asked what he thought of Astroturf, Tug said he didn't want to play on anything he couldn't smoke. "Some days you tame the tiger," he has said about his craft. "Other days the tiger has you for lunch." At a press conference announcing his retirement, Tug showed a highlights film of his greatest moments in baseball.

One of the premier relievers in baseball today is Dan Quisenberry, "a left-hander caught in a right-hander's body," as he was once described. "I don't want to be a 'celebrity,'" Quisenberry told Jim Murray. "I want to have regular neighbors. I want people to say 'How're your kids?' not 'How's your slider?' I don't want them peeking through the curtains and pointing at me to their relatives from out of town, I want them to borrow the lawn mower. I'm a quiet guy. I go to bed early at night. I want to have a listed phone and a station wagon and be able to hang around like everybody else."

Quiz might have gotten his wish to be a regular guy if he'd stayed much longer with a forkball as his out pitch. Abandoning the forkball after being knocked out of the box in back-to-back games, he said, "I stuck a fork in it and decided it was done." That may have been the time, as he explained, "I was Drano out there—right down the drain." Like many relievers, Quisenberry uses humor to get him through the bad days: "Probably so I can live with the memory of letting down another pitcher, the manager, the pitching coach, the GM, thirty-five thousand fans and my mom."

Yet another of these singular souls was Jim Kern, who described the non-stop excitement of being in the big leagues this way: "You read seven papers and don't remember a thing. You drink one hundred forty cups of coffee and go to the john after every thirtieth. Then maybe you go to a shopping mall and get lost. This life drives you crazy. I know. It drove me crazy two years ago and I never recovered." Kern may have hit on one of the traits common to all inhabitants of the bullpen. Said baseball executive Gabe Paul: "Relieving takes a fellow who is absolutely unafraid of the consequences, a fellow who has no fear. Being a little nuts goes along with that."

With all these fun-loving fellows sitting around, and all that time on their hands waiting for their number to be called (sometimes it never is), *something* has to break. Some blithe spirits have tried to order pizza from the bullpen phone. In intimate Wrigley Field, people in the seats sometimes share hot dogs and drinks with the bullpenners. At Fenway Park, Red Sox manager Don Zimmer called down to the pen to summon a young pitcher named (no kidding) Wilhelmus Remmerswaal. "Get Win up," Zimmer commanded, but was told that was impossible: "He's out in the bleachers buying peanuts."

Then there was the case of Will McEnaney. While in the minors in Indianapolis, he used to walk an imaginary dog outside the team dugout with an invisible leash. This made Vern Rapp, the manager, so mad that he snapped, "McEnaney, get that damned dog inside!" C. W. Nevius of the *San Francisco Chronicle* tells the story of how McEnaney wanted to catch an important Pittsburgh Steelers game on television. With Montreal at the time, McEnaney persuaded his twin brother to dress up in his Expos uniform and take his place in the bullpen while he stayed in the clubhouse watching football. When the call went out for Will—an unexpected development, as he wasn't supposed to pitch that day—his brother, a right-hander, started warming up. Unfortunately, Will was a left-hander. An irate Norm Sherry, the pitching coach, seeing a right-hander throwing instead of a lefty, phoned the bullpen back instantly. "If McEnaney's going to screw around," he shouted, "tell him to sit down!"

In Philadelphia, the catchers and relievers used to relieve themselves in a portable toilet set up in the bullpen. The Pirates were in town for a series and—well, we'll let Steve Nicosia, who was in on the gag, tell it:

"One time Ed Ott went in there and the guys turned it over on the door so he couldn't get out. They just left him.

The game was over and everybody left. Then the team was all sitting around the clubhouse eating the meal and somebody wanted to know where Ott was.

"'Oh yeah,' somebody said, 'maybe you ought to go out to the pen and get him. He's in the toilet.'"

Gone Hollywood

1
The Two Sides of Tommy

There's the Tommy Lasorda everyone knows—the man who bleeds Dodger blue, the chubby, effervescent loyalist and company man who, while managing Albuquerque in the minors, would tell his players going up to the big leagues, "When you get a hit and win a game in Dodger Stadium some day, just remember there's old Tom somewhere with a tear in his eye." This Tommy is as corny as Minnie Pearl with the price tag hanging off her hat. Speaking about the distinctiveness of the Dodger name, as opposed to other teams, he'll tell you, "If someone says, 'Hey I'm with the Indians,' I say, 'What reservation you from?' A guy told me the other day he was a Twin and I said, 'Yeah, where's your brother?'"

If you let him, this Tommy will crack jokes about his

swollen waistline: "When we were playing well last season, I was happy and ate a lot. When we were playing lousy, I got ·nervous and ate a lot." His celebrity status: "It's not worth much today," he said to a fan while signing his autograph, "but in five years it will be worth even less." And his perennial optimism: "I am the world's greatest optimist. The first was General George Custer. Surrounded by ten thousand Indians, he told his troops to take no prisoners." This Tommy hobnobs with celebrities like Frank Sinatra and Don Rickles and is often the target of the latter's jokes. Asked why he predicted the Dodgers to win the title, Rickles said, "Lasorda will have to win because Sinatra and I are holding his relatives hostage."

This is the Artful Dodger we have all come to know, yet there's a side of Lasorda not fit for family consumption. The man has the foulest mouth this side of Eddie Murphy. Oh boy, can this guy cuss. When he's on a tear the seven forbidden words aren't enough for him, he has to invent new ones. Tapes of his profanity-drenched locker-room tirades—the 1978 Dave Kingman is probably the most famous—are cult classics passed around the league among players and reporters. Maybe someone could do a video with them and Lasorda would have a whole new career.

The way it starts is a reporter, perhaps not so innocently, asks the Dodger manager what he thinks of a given development in a game. In the case of Kingman, the Mets slugger had just hit three humongous home runs to beat LA. "What did I think of them?" said Lasorda, astonished that someone would ask him such a question. "You saw those fuckin' balls. What the fuck do you think of those fuckin'"—and off he went on a twenty-minute rant that would've made Leo Durocher blush.

In spring training one year, after sitting through a comparable Lasorda diatribe, Don Sutton passed his manager a note: "Congratulations. You have just set a world record by using the same word one hundred seventy-one times in fifteen minutes." Lasorda responded, "Yeah, and I ain't even got to fuckin' Jay Johnstone yet for driving onto the fuckin' practice field on his fuckin' motorcycle—" and he launched off afresh, or in this case, afoul.

One concluding anecdote perhaps best shows the dual Lasorda personality—part Mister Rogers, part Falstaff. In the locker room before an important Sunday game, Lasorda stood up to address the team and give them a pep talk. Yet he seemed unusually serious, a somber expression on his face as if he were about to confess his sins.

"Men, you're always hearing me use bad language," he said with emotion, "but today you're going to hear the real me." Then Lasorda read a passage from the Bible that he said was a personal favorite. Whenever he felt down or things seemed to be going bad in the world, he read from the Scriptures. And the passage Lasorda read struck a chord with the team, for the locker room became absolutely still. Everyone in the room that day was moved—almost to tears, some say—and it was left for their leader, the man with the Bible, to break the quiet.

"All right, you guys," Tommy said. "Now I want you to go out there and kick the living shit out of those mother-fuckers!"

2
Headhunter

Speaking of image transformations, even Tommy Lasorda (and his agent) could learn a thing or two from the job that's been done on Don Drysdale, who, since retiring from pitching, has become a game announcer and a play-by-play man for ABC's *Monday Night Baseball*. The image Drysdale projects on the air is that of Little John, an affable big guy with a heart of gold, a kind, sweet soul who would walk around an ant in his way rather than step on it. But on the playing field the Big D was anything but sweet; he was a merciless competitor, a man who did not shy from using the baseball in his hand as a weapon of intimidation in his war with the hitter. (Drysdale's counterpart in football broad-casting is Merlin Olsen, another pro athlete with strong LA connections who has undergone an image makeover to make his persona more palatable to mainstream television au-diences. Olsen, who busted heads while a defensive tackle for the Rams' Fearsome Foursome, has been selling flowers on TV, for chrissakes.)

At six foot five, Drysdale was a pitching descendant of old Burleigh Grimes who, one observer said, always looked as if he was about to commit assault and battery with the ball, and Sal Maglie, beanball artist for the New York Gi-ants. It was, in fact, the master Maglie who advised the young Drysdale to throw not just one knockdown pitch, but two—"because the second one makes the hitter know you meant the first."

The pupil learned his lessons well, slicing at hitters' heads with a vengeance and skill unknown even to the great beanball executioners of the past. Nobody in modern Na-tional League history has more hit-batsmen scalps than Drysdale. Jimmy Cannon wrote, "Rage once deprived him of his talent. He would walk a guy and the rage against himself would make him wilder or he would start throwing at batters. Anger blinded him and he couldn't see the plate. Once the other team had ten men, because he was arrayed against himself."

This rage, however it may have held Drysdale back, also worked in his favor, sending a fearful, doom-laden message to hitters around the league. Better not dig in too deep—and if you do, get ready to duck. Cognizant of the edge his knockdown pitch—or more subtly, the *threat* of it—gave him, Drysdale rode it all the way to the Hall of Fame. In a game against the Braves he hit Henry Aaron in the back with a pitch. The next day, during the pregame warm-up, the two men met again at the batting cage.

"Sorry I hit you in the back yesterday," Drysdale told Aaron. "I meant to hit you in the neck."

Sex and the Single
(or Married) Ballplayer;
or, Are We Not Men?

"There are only three kinds of women in this world: givers, takers and destroyers," said the pitcher Bo Belinsky. "You really have to watch out for those destroyers."

"You have to do tobacco like you do women," said infielder Phil Garner. "You must let it work up to a good chew, let it get moist and juicy. If you chew too fast, it'll become dry and fall apart."

Cliff Johnson, explaining why he sometimes kisses his bat before hitting: "I do that when I need something. It's like with your wife. If you want something from her, you butter her up."

Jim Bouton, instructing his teammates as they were about to meet their wives at the airport after a road trip (presumably one that had lots of extramarital sex): "All right you guys, look horny!"

The attitudes of major league ballplayers toward women can roughly be grouped into two major categories: 1) the kind of prankish, schoolboy foolishness exposed by Bouton in *Ball Four* (and subsequent volumes by him and others), in which players typically satisfy adolescent fantasies by searching the stands with their eyes looking for the best beaver shots; and 2) the cooler, more macho stance of the big, bad hombre who swings a big stick and makes big bucks and don't you dig it, baby. "There are two things you can't change about a man," said Al Oliver, speaking for hot-strutting ballplayers everywhere. "His sex and his pride." When Denny McLain, who's got his own problems, was asked how he was going to celebrate after winning his thirtieth game in a season, he said, "I'm going home and have a couple cool ones. Then my wife and I will think of something."

The wife in baseball circles is, if you will, a kind of

straight man, a Bud Abbott or Dan Rowan character that ballplayers and baseball personalities can make the butt of their jokes. Joked Joe Garagiola, "I know a baseball star who wouldn't report the theft of his wife's credit cards because the thief spends less than she does." "For most ballplayers," Don Kowet wrote, "all getting married means is that now they have to hide their date books." Asked the most difficult thing about the major leagues, Mike Hegan said, "Explaining to your wife why *she* needs a penicillin shot for your kidney infection." After husband Pete signed a three-million-plus contract with Philadelphia, Karolyn Rose supposedly asked, "Do they have a K Mart there?"

Apocryphal wife stories are about as common as Yogi Berra yarns and, considering the audience they're playing to, as certain a laugh-getter. After Lefty Gomez was knocked out of the box in the opening game of a doubleheader, his wife counseled him: "Don't worry, honey. Maybe you'll win the second game." While the reported first conversation between Kent and Linda Tekulve—

KENT: "Hi there. I'm a baseball player."
LINDA: "Oh really? Well, I follow baseball."
KENT: "You do? What's your favorite team?"
LINDA: "Oh, I don't know. The, uh, Chicago Dodgers."

—is a classic, if kindly, tale illustrating a common wifely trait (in the minds of baseball men), ignorance.

But the women can—and do—jab back. Author Bob Chieger reports on good authority that Paula Bouton, ex-wife of Jim Bouton, really did say after watching her first-ever baseball game, "I'm not sure what it means, but whenever the ball is not in play, somebody grabs his crotch."

For that matter, baseball wives may not be as innocent as their husbands would like to believe. In the words of one, "Some of those players would be a little shocked if they knew what the little ladies were doing back home when they were on the road."

ADDENDUM

In case any youngsters get the impression that the majors are completely filled with philanderers and men of loose morals (would you believe ninety percent?), a footnote should be added about an old-time speedball pitcher who was reputed to be quite the swinger himself. That is, until he met a certain Miss Janet Howard. Miss Howard was working as a waitress in a Pittsburgh restaurant when Satchel Paige, then barnstorming around the country as the star attraction in the Negro Leagues, came in for a bite to eat. It was love at first sight.

"From the minute she first set a plate of asparagus down in front of me," said Satchel, "I began to feel paralyzed." They were married shortly thereafter.

Reggie

Years ago a woman was struck by a car and was lying, in pain, on her back in a Manhattan street. A Good Samaritan yelled at passersby to call the police and then rushed up to the woman's side to give her comfort.

"Don't be afraid," the Samaritan said to her. "My name is Reggie Jackson and everybody in this city knows me."

Without exception, no player of his generation has received as much hectoring, criticism and outright ridicule as Reggie Jackson. It is the result of his overpowering desire, especially when younger, to be center stage at all times, to be the straw that stirs the drink. "Reggie Jackson has never done anything in his life that was not for effect," said Bill Lee, who pitched against him for the Red Sox. "He's a total phony," said Thurman Munson. Added Billy Martin, "I never wanted Reggie batting cleanup for me. I wanted Chris Chambliss. Reggie might be Mr. October, but Chambliss—that guy was Mr. Season."

Reggie's poor fielding—"He made more errors in one season than I made in my entire career," carped Jimmy Piersall—is seen as a product of his massive ego, characteristic of a man of great natural talents who won't work to overcome his weaknesses. And his famous home run act, the way he drops his bat and stands at the plate to watch the flight of the ball, followed by his lumbering trot around the bases—all this is derided as show biz, a hotdog play to the fans and, as always, his personal conceit. Said pitcher Don Sutton, "I object to guys who trot the bases like they have saved the world from utter chaos."

Off the field, he gets it too. In an auto accident in New York City a few years ago, the man whom Reggie collided with pulled a gun out and fired a volley of shots over Jackson's head. Said a rival player at the time, "It had to be *over* his head. If it was at his head, they couldn't have missed."

To a great extent Reggie himself brings on this criticism, even invites it. The guy is certainly a pop-off. Told the crosstown New York Mets had drawn only a few thousand people to an afternoon game, Reggie, then with the Yankees, said, "Shoot, I could draw that many by having batting practice on a Monday afternoon." To criticism of his stumbling play in the field, he replied: "Fielding? There are lots of guys who can catch a baseball. I make a million dollars with my bat." Eyeing the short left field wall at Fenway Park, he said, "If I played here my whole career, they would've named a whole candy counter after me"—a comment not unlike another he made when asked if he'd ever consider playing in Japan: "If I did, they'd name a box of rice after me."

Reggie became REG–GIE! REG–GIE! REG–GIE!— capital letters, exclamation points, fans chanting in unison— during his years as a New York Yankee. Among other things, he hit three absolutely glorious home runs in a World Series game, rising above a time that, like his previous stint with the Charlie Finley–owned A's, was chock-full of fights, controversy, bitterness, hard feelings. If Reggie cannot take full blame for the acrimony that pervaded the Yankee clubhouse in those years, he deserves a goodly share.

There was Reggie as crybaby, the unappreciated hero demanding to be traded: "I'll just call Federal Express and say I got a big package waiting for them."

There was Reggie as martyr, Reggie with a persecution complex as big as the outfield at Yankee Stadium: "I'm the hunted on the team that is being hunted. They're looking for me, but I'll handle it like a big dog." And: "It's uncomfortable being me, it's uncomfortable being considered something I'm not, an idol or a monster, something hated or loved."

After being suspended, Jackson's return to the Stadium was met by a torrent of boos, except for a small group in the right field stands who did not join in. Explained Reggie: "All the fans in those sections are black, under ten, and don't read the newspapers." Jackson was seen as the villain of the team—creating bad vibes with his self-superior bluster, setting a bad example with his lack of hustle, chiding teammates. After Fred Stanley, the weak-hitting shortstop, was set down by a pitcher just brought up from the minors, Reggie mocked him: "Man, that guy doesn't even have a baseball card and he got you out." Ed Linn reported that Jackson once sat at the front of the team bus, in full view of his teammates, counting out one-hundred-dollar bills from his wallet. His two favorite topics of conversation were money and his allegedly great intellect. "What am I arguing with you for?" Jackson screamed at Mickey Rivers during a clubhouse argument. "You can't read or write." Said Rivers: "You better stop reading and start hitting!"

There are any number of reasons why Jackson had such trouble with the Yankees, indeed with everybody throughout his career. (With the Angels he has mellowed somewhat, enjoying the approbations deserving of a star in the sunset of his career.) But what saved him as a player may also have been what caused so many people to dislike him: He produced. Nothing galls people so much as a man who does what he says. "Reggie is a charlatan, but a charlatan with credentials," Don Sutton said. "He cons people and sells himself, but he produces." Reggie, in the grand manner of Babe Ruth, called his shots. After coming to New York he *did* get a candy bar named after him, per his prediction. He took his own advice—"Hit the ball over the wall. Then everything takes care of itself"—and in the process came to embody, like a reigning heavyweight champ, the foolishness, the excesses, the aspirations of his time. No statistics can convey what he communicated at the plate: that sense of rising excitement, that sense of a great possibility opening up before us, an opportunity waiting to be seized— and when he connected and the ball took off, our joy at seeing it hit by a man who got as much pleasure out of it as we do.

The story is told of a young woman who came to visit New York City for the first time. Deathly afraid of what might happen to her alone in the big city, she took every conceivable precaution to guard her safety. She carried only the minimum of cash. She never went out at night. She stayed away from the subways.

On the night before the woman was scheduled to leave the city, she got on the hotel elevator to go up to her room.

At the fifth floor the elevator stopped, and a large black man, holding a ferocious-looking Doberman pinscher by a leash, stepped into the car with her.

"Lay down!" the man said, and the woman, terrified at the sight of the man and the dog, lay down on the floor of the elevator, as instructed. But, to her relief and surprise, nothing happened. The man and his dog got off two floors up.

The next morning, the woman found a note in her box in the lobby as she was checking out. It read,

"Thank you for giving me the biggest laugh of my life. (Signed) Reggie Jackson."

A man like that will go in the Hall of Fame on the first ballot, laughing all the way.

7
Seventh Inning Stretch

"Just as she said this, she noticed that one of the trees had a door leading right into it. 'That's very curious!' she thought. 'But everything's curious today. I think I may as well go in at once.'"

—LEWIS CARROLL, *Alice's Adventures in Wonderland*

A Conversation with Danny Ozark*

Q: HELLO, SPORTS FANS, and thank you for joining us for another edition of *Sports Talk Radio* on WIZZ in Indianapolis, Indiana. We're talking here tonight with Danny Ozark, who needs no introduction to baseball fans around the country. He's been in baseball all his life, and now he's coaching for the Los Angeles Dodgers. Tell us, Danny, how are the Dodgers shaping up this season?

DANNY OZARK: We have a lot of new players, but not many.

Q: I see. Now you've been both a coach and a manager, Danny. To what do your attribute your success?

OZARK: I have good repertory with my players.

Q: We'll grant you that, Danny, but always? What about that '78 Phillies team you managed. You won your division that year but the Dodgers dumped on you in the Championship Series. What do you say about that?

OZARK: Look. Even Napoleon had his Watergate.

Q: Tell me, Danny. Do you remember what you said back then—

OZARK *(interrupting):* I don't want to get into any Galphonse-Aston act with you.

Q: That's understandable. But—

OZARK: Listen, I will not be cohorsed.

Q: Okay, okay Danny, cool down. I don't blame you for

---

* This is an imaginary conversation, but every word spoken by Ozark and the other interviewees is their own. They have all said these things, though not in this context.

being touchy about the subject. But that Phillies team definitely had morale problems, wouldn't you agree?

OZARK: The team's morality is no factor.

Q: Hey, look who's here! Now that's what I call timing. Ladies and gentlemen, Johnny Logan has just come into our studio. What a nice surprise. Johnny of course is the ex-Braves shortstop who's since become a fine broadcaster in his own right. Thanks for dropping in on us tonight, Johnny.

JOHNNY LOGAN: My pleasure. And thank you for recognizing my intangibles.

Q: It's only right, Johnny. Your broadcasting style is one of the finest in the game, right up there with Jerry Coleman's. How would you characterize your broadcast technique?

LOGAN: It's sort of like Lou Boudreau. He does a good job of recapping the play before it happens.

Q: Excuse me, fellas. Have you two been introduced? Johnny Logan, have you met Danny Ozark?

LOGAN: I know the name but I can't replace the face.

Q: Well, then. Johnny, I don't know if you were listening outside, but Danny and I were discussing the '78 Phillies and how much trouble they had when he was their manager.

LOGAN: Well, you know, Rome wasn't born in a day.

Q *(in an excited voice):* Oh no! I can't believe it! This is incredible! They told me we'd be having some unexpected guests drop in, but this is too much. First Danny Ozark and Johnny Logan, and now the great Yogi Berra here in our studio! What a show this is turning out to be. Yogi, Yogi, sit down. Have a seat anywhere. And thanks for coming down.

YOGI BERRA: Thank you for making this night necessary.

Q: Gee, I just can't get over it. The one and only Yogi Berra, here on WIZZ, the happy voice of Indianapolis. Did you know Yogi was here, Johnny?

LOGAN: I heard his footprints coming down the hall.

Q: Oh, I get it. You guys were all hiding out downstairs, watching TV. What was on?

LOGAN: They've got this new Shakespearean play on, *McBride*. It's got a lot of suspension.

Q: Is that so? Well, I know for a fact that Yogi Berra is one baseball man who appreciates culture and the arts. I was reading about your recent trip to Paris, Yogi. How'd you enjoy the Louvre?

YOGI: It's okay if you like paintings.

Q: And what about the opera. We heard you saw *Tosca*. What'd you think?

YOGI: It was pretty good. Even the music.

Q: That's great, Yog. But let's turn to baseball, shall we? I've got a million things I want to ask you.

YOGI: If you ask me anything I don't know, I'm not going to answer.

Q: Does that include the '73 World Series? You were managing the Mets then, and the A's, led by Bert Campaneris and Sal Bando, beat your boys in seven games. Care to comment?

YOGI: I don't know anything at all about that Blando and Campanis.

Q: Okay, suit yourself. Tell you what, Yogi. We'll play some free association. You know how that works? I'll throw out some names, and you say whatever pops into your mind.

YOGI: Okay.

Q: You're sure now? The first thing that comes into your mind. Got it?

YOGI: Yeah, sure. Go ahead.

Q: Okay, here we go then. Mickey Mantle.

YOGI: What about him?

Q *(fumbling at the microphone):* "Uh, well, okay Yogi. But I tell you, all you people out there in radio land, sometimes I feel like I've got my feet on the ground as far as my head is concerned, know what I mean? *(Pause.)* Oh well, maybe Danny Ozark can straighten it all out for us. Tell us, Danny, what does it all mean?

OZARK: It's beyond my apprehension.

Q: Oh my, it's time for a short commercial break. After

that we'll come back and take calls, and all of you can have your chance to talk with Yogi, Johnny and Danny. Is anybody out there? I don't see our phone board lighting up. Callers, help us out. We need you. Callers, are you there? Callers?

Quintessences

Walter Johnson was so fast "he could throw three strikes at a time," said Ogden Nash.

Ryne Duren was so wild that he hit Billy Hunter with a pitch while Hunter was waiting in the on-deck circle.

Dick Radatz threw twenty-seven straight balls in a spring training game.

The young Eddie Murray had such a perfect swing that the first time Earl Weaver saw him bat, he decided to keep him on the Orioles.

Catcher Frank Grant was so eager to play that he shimmied eight feet up a telegraph pole to catch a pop foul.

Babe Ruth could fart at will.

Cool Papa Bell could shave on a moving bus.

Reggie Jackson hit a home run with such force that it was in the seats before the right fielder even had a chance to move.

As a boy, Paul Waner learned to hit by using corncobs.

When Greg Luzinski was fourteen, he could hit a baseball over three hundred and fifty feet.

Jim Rice is so strong that he has broken his bat simply by checking his swing.

The submarine delivery of pitcher Carl Mays was so low that he sometimes scraped his knuckles on the ground as he threw.

Tom Seaver was warming up on a damp day in Riverfront Stadium. After he finished, the groundskeeper came out to rake the mound and found only two footprints.

Seaver's feet had landed in the same spot every time he pitched.

Don Larsen threw so slow his pitches "ought to have been equipped with backup lights," said Shirley Povich.

Beanballer Early Wynn was so mean that "he'd knock you down in the dugout," according to Mickey Mantle.

Joe Black threw a duster at a batter who hit the ground so quickly that the ball sailed between his head and his flying cap.

Bill Terry, said Dizzy Dean, "hit a ball between my legs so hard that my center fielder caught it on the fly backing up against the wall."

Dave Kingman hit a pop fly so high it vanished in the pillow roofing at the Metrodome.

Bill Reddy swears that Duke Snider used to hit pop flies so high that the second baseman had time to pull a magazine out of his back pocket and read an article before they would come back down to land.

Jackie Robinson tagged up and scored from first on a sacrifice fly.

Ty Cobb, angry at the opposing team's manager, fouled off sixteen straight pitches into its dugout.

"One old-time player," says Billy Crystal, "was so fast that he could hit a line drive through the box and the ball would hit him in the back as he was sliding into second."

"Envision, if you will, an auto speeding on a pier, braking at the last moment and then plunging over the side into the drink."—Ron Fimrite, on the split-fingered fastball of Bruce Sutter.

Ducky Medwick hit a home run off a pitched ball that was so high and wild that the catcher said he couldn't have caught it if Medwick had let it go by.

Ernie Banks hit a home run off the first pitch he saw in his first-ever at bat on the opening day of spring training in his rookie year in the majors.

Thirteen Reasons Why Baseball, Not Football, Is the Game of the Eighties (and Beyond)

1. Football stinks. Baseball is great.
2. Baseball is the people's game. How often do you see someone wear a football helmet on the street? But people wear the caps of their favorite baseball team on the street all the time.

   Furthermore, how often does the president of the United States throw out the ceremonial first football of the season? Oh, you may get a schlócky, media-contrived presidential flip of the coin, as in Super Bowl XIX. But presidents have been throwing out the first ball of the baseball season since Taft (or was it McKinley?).
3. Football zealots cite superior attendance figures and high TV ratings as proof of their game's greater popularity. Baloney. Who wants to be seen with the type of people who go to football games anyway? You're always elbow to elbow, the lout behind you has probably spilled beer down your neck, and the lines to the men's rooms are a mile long.

   Baseball, on the other hand, is civilized. By late August you can pick a game between, say, the Giants and the Pirates, or the Indians and Rangers, and you won't have to worry about crowds. Chances are there'll be more people waiting at your corner bus stop than attending these games. Hell, management may be so glad to see you they'll park your car for you. And you can get to know your hot dog vendor and beer salesman personally.
4. Baseball has the bleachers. Indeed, what other sport has an institution comparable to the bleachers, ex-

cept for maybe the grandstands in horse racing. God bless the bleachers, where a guy can still see a game, get drunk, and get in a fight all for a measly few bucks.

5. Baseball has a history. What does football have but Roman numerals? Baseball, or some version of it, predates the Civil War. Like so many of our finest traditions, such as parliamentary democracy and *The Benny Hill Show,* it comes from England.

    And where does football come from? A bunch of prehistoric preppies rolling around in the mud in New Jersey or some place like that. It's college-boy stuff. Rah rah sis boom bah.

6. Baseball is an international sport. They play baseball in the U.S., Puerto Rico, Canada, Mexico, Japan, Latin America, the Caribbean, Cuba, Nicaragua and Oakland. Where do they play American football but in America? They don't even play pro football in Oakland anymore. (Not unless you count the USFL. But who cares about them?)

7. Baseball does not have Al Davis, Pete Rozelle, a clock, the boring point-after-touchdown kick, half-time shows, marching bands, Brent Musburger, Robert Irsay, tailgate parties, the crackback block, Army vs. Navy, Jack Tatum, Jack Kemp, television time-outs, Donald Trump and Super Bowl Week. Then again, football does not have George Steinbrenner. Call it a toss-up.

8. Anybody ever hear of football trading cards? "I'll give you my Lyle Alzado and Joe Klecko for your Joe Montana . . ." Naw, it just doesn't work.

9. Baseball is a game of nuance. Most football fans don't even know what "nuance" means.

10. Baseball is every day. Football is only the weekends (and Monday nights if it's a good game). Unless the players are on strike, you can get your baseball fix almost every day, unlike football. Football is all

foreplay; it strings you out with six days of hype before (yawn) delivering the goods. Speaking of hype,

11. Compare the Super Bowl with the World Series. For the Super Bowl we get enough hype to kill a tribe of elephants, and nine times out of ten, the game's a yawner. We probably get as much hype during the Series, but at least we get six or seven games to digest it.

12. Okay, admittedly football is better on TV, but which game would you rather watch in person? Football? Be serious. No matter how they try to gussy it up with militaristic lingo and Roman gladiator music on the postgame shows, football is still . . . *football.*

13. Finally, the reason baseball is the greatest game of all is its fans. Baseball fans are not the type of people who enjoy seeing halfbacks disabled. They are classy, intelligent, literate, passionately devoted to their game, and above all, reasonable.

8

Out in Left Field: A Gaggle of Characters in Search of a Game

"A flake is a natural thing from the clouds."
—GEORGE THEODORE, former Met

Crazy Rube

RUBE WADDELL once left a game in progress to chase a fire truck. He was, in the words of an ex-teammate, "just an overgrown boy." Between innings during a game he could occasionally be found playing marbles under the stands with the local kids. Parades fascinated him. If one was in town, Rube might skip the game that day to go watch or maybe even join in the marching. Who cared if he was pitching? His manager and teammates certainly, but not Rube.

Wilfrid Sheed in *The Ultimate Baseball Book* called Waddell one of the "dim-witted roustabouts . . . who were the very essence of baseball in those days, if you could get them to show up." Attendance was definitely not one of the big left-hander's strong points. He might pitch a game, then disappear for three or four days without bothering to inform anyone of his whereabouts. Fishing was a favorite pastime— he reportedly took off for ten days on a fishing trip in the middle of a season—as was playing pickup games down at the corner sandlot.

When Waddell did show up at the park, it was often at the last minute and with great dramatic effect. Minutes before a big game he was scheduled to pitch, someone would spot him coming through the stands, and seemingly every head in the place would turn to look. Jumping onto the field, he would tear off his shirt as he walked toward the clubhouse to change his clothes. When he reappeared later to take his warm-up pitches, the crowd would go nuts.

"You couldn't control him 'cause he was just a big kid himself," Sam Crawford told Lawrence Ritter. "Baseball was just a game to Rube." Part showman, part child, he used to pour ice water on his pitching arm before games. The reason, he said, was to slow himself down so he didn't "burn up" the catcher's mitt. Rube banged up his shoulder in a tussle with a teammate over a straw hat. He never wore underwear. He was also something of a roustabout. Jimmy Austin recalled hitting a homer off Waddell, who was so drunk that as he turned dizzily in a circle to watch Austin round the bases, he fell flat on his butt.

Waddell's best years as a pitcher came with Connie Mack's Philadelphia A's in the early 1900s. Like some other baseball individualists that came after him, people speculated on how good the lackadaisical lefty could have been if he had really applied himself. As it was he made the Hall of Fame on the strength of an overpowering fastball and curve. Branch Rickey said, "When Waddell had control—and some sleep—he was unbeatable." One team found that out after a fan in the stands hit Waddell in the head with an egg. Not losing his temper, Rube called in his outfielders and, like Satchel Paige after him, struck out the side. He walked off the field with the crowd cheering.

Waddell died in 1914, at the age of thirty-seven. Even then, he was seen as an anachronism, his simple boyish antics the relic of another, more innocent time that had long since faded into the past. He was an overgrown kid who had the impish audacity to see the emperor without any clothes. Baseball was a fun thing to Rube, a game. "In his life he gave a lot of people a lot of enjoyment," said Jimmy Austin. The *Literary Digest* wrote, "He was one of those characters at once the most enviable and the saddest and most pitiful in the world, who are too great at heart for the civilization in which they live. They are affectionate, good-hearted giants."

Loverboy

"I have no regrets, not one. I was there. I saw it and did it all. I heard music nobody else ever heard," Bo Belinsky

said after he retired, and a look back at his career may
explain why the pitcher had so few regrets. Bo *did* do it all, if
not on the field then off it. "There is a race to Bo Belinsky's
pad every morning," a sportswriter remarked. "It is a race
to see who arrives there first, Belinsky or his milkman. Belinsky has yet to win."

After winning his first six starts for the Angels in his
rookie season, including a no-hitter against Baltimore, Bo
was off to the races. He sported about southern California in
a Cadillac convertible, hustled pool games, and dated the
prettiest Hollywood starlets. "I like his body," a minor
league scout once said of Belinsky, and many young women
came to agree. He was Casanova with a curveball, a man
whose biggest triumphs came after the game was over. Even
his mother back in New York seemed to wink approval:
"He's out in Malibu Beach now," she told a reporter. "That
ain't Coney Island, you know."

With his movie-star good looks and freewheeling lifestyle, Bo quickly became a favorite of the not–Coney Island
crowd. Walter Winchell, the gossip columnist, befriended
him, and his visibility around town increased still more. He
proposed to Mamie Van Doren, who was to Marilyn
Monroe what Belinsky was to Joe DiMaggio. But their en-
gagement soon broke off, the actress sending his ring back in
a huff. "He bought it on credit and needs the money," she
sniped. Bo didn't look back though, eventually marrying a
former Playmate of the Year.

Another playboy of that era, New York's Joe Pepitone,
told Howard Cosell, "I discovered the city, the Copa and all
that. I found I could hit .996 on the street. It probably took
sixty points off my average." If Belinsky were a hitter, the
comment could neatly encapsulate his own years as a pro.
Outside the boudoir, his fortunes fizzled like a dud fire-
cracker. After his sensational '62 start he lost more games
than he won that year and his reputation as a late-night
rambler caught up with him. "He's got a million-dollar arm
and a ten-cent head," was one description of him that made
the rounds. After a ruckus in the Angels clubhouse, a coach

told him, "When anything goes wrong around here, Belinsky, you're the first one I suspect."

For his part, Bo had little patience for authority figures of any type. "We hit it off immediately," he said of one of his managers. "He hated me and I hated him." Belinsky had to learn the hard way what others before and after him have come to realize—that in baseball what you do on the field may not necessarily be as important as what you do off it. Bo pitched for a handful of teams and was out of the game in eight years.

Yet he shall be remembered, not for his win-loss record, but for his remarkable pre- and postgame performances with the opposite sex. Though these days Bo plays down his enduring reputation as a sexual athlete. "If I did everything they said I did," he has said, "I'd be in a jar at the Harvard Medical School."

Yogi

One time Yogi Berra did a radio interview show with sportscaster Jack Buck, after which he received a check made out to "Pay to Bearer." Yogi was hurt. "Hey Jack," he said, "you've known me all these years. And you still don't know how to spell my name?"

On a broiling hot summer day in New York City in the late sixties, a reception in honor of the Yankees was held at Gracie Mansion, the mayor's residence. Yogi Berra, looking dapper, strolled in late, catching the eye of the mayor's wife. "My, you certainly look cool today," she said to him. "Why thank you," Yogi replied, "you don't look so hot yourself."

On hearing that a Jewish lord mayor had been elected in Dublin, Yogi said, "That's great. A thing like that could only happen in America."

Asked what he'd do if he found a million dollars on the street, Yogi said, "I'd see if I could find the guy who lost it, and if he was poor, I'd give it back to him."

Somebody once accused him of being a fatalist. "You

mean I save postage stamps?" Yogi said. "Not on your life."

Yogi, to a slumping batter: "Swing only at the strikes."

One hitter under Yogi's tutelage was trying to imitate the batting stance of Hall of Famer Frank Robinson. "If you can't imitate him," Yogi told the youngster, "don't copy him."

On a road trip with the Yankees Berra found the bed in his room uncomfortable. He went downstairs and told the clerk, "I tried sleeping standing up, but the pillow kept falling."

Asked for his reaction after his career homer mark for catchers was broken, Yogi said, "I always thought the record would stand until it was broken."

On a former classmate of his: "He was so popular in school, nobody could stand him."

"I never like to golf in the morning and get involved in a ball game at night," Yogi has said. "I don't like to think twice in the same day."

One year during the World Series Berra took the subway to Brooklyn, explaining, "I knew I was gonna take the wrong train, so I left early."

In the market for a new home, Yogi was shown a huge, turn-of-the-century mansion. "What a house!" he exclaimed. "Nothin' but rooms!"

Yogi, in a clubhouse pep talk to his team: "You give one hundred percent in the first half of the game, and if that isn't enough, in the second half you give what's left."

Yogi said he had no problem managing the Yankees with George Steinbrenner and Billy Martin in the front office overseeing him: "After all, four heads are better than one."

At a White House dinner Yogi and his wife Carmen sat at the same table with King Fahd of Saudi Arabia and President Reagan. "The President chatted with the King a lot," Yogi said afterward. "I guess they've got a pretty good business going."

On the same dinner: "I thought they said steak dinner, but then I found out it was a state dinner."

At a crowded restaurant: "It was hard to have a conversation with anyone, there were so many people talking."

Berra sometimes played left field for New York in Yankee Stadium, where the afternoon sun shone directly into his eyes. He commented after one game, "It sure gets late early out there."

At a banquet for touring American ballplayers in Tokyo, the host was announcing the menu, an array of Japanese delicacies. Yogi raised his hand and said, "Don't you have any bread?"

When the Yankees acquired the speedy Rickey Henderson, manager Berra said, "He can run anytime he wants. I'm giving him the red light."

In the minors Yogi roomed with a young infielder, Bobby Brown, who went on to become a physician and president of the American League. One evening the two were relaxing in their room after a game. Brown, prepping for an exam he was about to take, was studying the medical text *Boyd's Pathology,* while Yogi was absorbed in a comic book. Both men happened to finish reading at the same time. As Brown closed his book, Yogi asked, "How did yours come out?"

Toots the Bartender

For years and years Toots Shor ran the best drinking establishment in New York City. Everybody from presidents to heavyweight champs drank there. Ernest Hemingway was known to frequent the place, along with movie stars and glitterati of all shades. "Through booze," Toots said, "I met two chief justices, fifty world champs, six presidents and DiMaggio and Babe Ruth."

Toots loved sports of all kinds, but especially baseball. "I don't know if I'm making a mistake," he was quoted as saying, "but I'm raising my kid as a Giants fan." Though respectful of the dominating team in the Bronx, Toots subscribed to the famous Jimmy Cannon line about fan loyalty in the Big Apple: "The Giants were *our* team. We staked the tourists to the Yankees." After the Giants went west Shor's allegiances shifted in time to the clumsy new kids on the block, the Casey Stengel–led Mets, who astounded the world in the early sixties with their all-time horrific play. "I have a son," Toots told Jimmy Breslin, "and I make him watch the Mets. I want him to know life. You watch the Mets . . . it's a history lesson. He'll understand the Depression when they teach it to him in school."

The next time you're in a bar or at home knocking back a few with the game on the tube, think of Toots. Here was a great baseball fan on the order of that Philadelphia newspaperman who, when a local resident won a ho-hum scientific award in 1980, headlined the story of his achievement: PHILLIES FAN WINS NOBEL PRIZE.

Toots Shor would have appreciated this sentiment. He had a proper view of the role of baseball in society. Nobel Prizes are one thing, but when you're talking pennant races and the World Series, now that's *serious*. One evening at his bar Toots was sitting at a table with a group of people that included Sir Alexander Fleming, the discoverer of penicillin. In the door came Mel Ott, the great Giants power hitter, and Toots quickly got up.

"Pardon me," he said, "but I have to go. Somebody important just came in."

The Gozzlehead

You have to hand it to guys like Mickey Rivers, the man they called "The Gozzlehead." Wherever he played, wherever he went, he remained undeniably (and some say, unfortunately) his own man. One of his managers asked him once if he could help the team out by stealing more bases. Mickey said no way: "I'm going to pace myself and play for a good situation, 'cause if you hit that ground a hundred and fifty times a year, you got to be paining at the end of the year." The manager walked away paining.

Next to Rivers, Willie Montañez looked like Pete Rose. Mickey was known not to run out grounders if he was feeling in a bad mood. The Yankees wanted him to bunt more, but Old Man Rivers felt no obligation to do so. "If you don't want my habits, then trade me," he told Yankee management. "I ain't gonna work on my weaknesses 'cause it don't do any good." His manager, Billy Martin, had to threaten to beat Rivers up to get him to hustle more.

In his time Rivers may have had the weakest outfield arm in baseball; his throws, it was observed, packed all the wallop of a baby's burp. When he came up to the plate to hit he walked on the balls of his feet; Sparky Lyle said it looked as if Rivers "walked on coals for a living."

Mickey was not what you call a great thinker. "I got a higher IQ than you," he told Carlos May in a stormy Yankee clubhouse meeting. "Shit," replied May, "you can't even spell IQ." Asked his goals for the upcoming season, Rivers said, "Hit .300, score a hundred runs, and stay injury-prone." Here are a few more Mickeyisms (supplied by Peter Gammons of *The Sporting News*):

• "Mark Wagner looked lost out there at shortstop. He looked like the Lost Mohegan."

• "It was so cold today that I saw a dog chasing a cat and the dog was walking. The wind was blowing a hundred degrees."

• Instructing some kids on how to play the outfield: "The first thing you do when you get out to center field is put your finger up and check the wind-chill factor."

Celebrated for his flash and shine, Rivers was the kind of dude who could wear rhinestone socks and feel good about it. He liked all the social vices—women, drink, and gambling in particular. He reportedly asked to be traded from the Rangers because the only thing to bet on in Texas was the cockfights.

His release from the Rangers, ending his major league career, was a blow to lovers of baseball exotica and to Rivers personally. A long-standing ambition of his was to return to New York, where he had his best days, and be reunited with George Steinbrenner and Billy Martin on the Yankees. As Mickey explained, "George and Billy and me are two of a kind."

Another Immortal Babe

As John Lardner wrote, Babe Herman "did not always catch fly balls on the top of his head, but he could do it in a pinch." A free swinger with real punch in his bat, the Babe was a blunderbuss of monumental proportions in the outfield. He was a league-leading error-maker who, it was said, made sensational catches of easy fly balls. After being traded to the Dodgers, Fresco Thompson was given a locker next to Herman's. "Hell," snarled Herman. "They're making me dress next to a .250 hitter." "Hell," Thompson snarled back. "They're making me dress next to a .250 fielder."

That was not that far off the mark. A big, floppy-eared lunk from Buffalo, the Babe, whose given name was Floyd Caves but who should've been called "Klutz," infuriated managers with his sloppy fielding. But his base-hit bat gave him the leverage (or so he thought) to hold out for more money at contract time. His frequent holdouts in turn ticked off his bosses, who passed him around the league like so many mashed potatoes.

Throughout all the Babe was unflappable. Late in 1926, his rookie season, Herman hadn't stolen any bases, which caused his manager, Wilbert Robinson, to ask: "What's the matter, can't you steal?" And the Babe said, "Steal? Why hell, you never asked me to."

Perhaps Herman knew something Uncle Robbie did not, for legend has it that the Babe once tried to steal third with the bases loaded. In another misadventure, Herman slashed a hard liner to right. Seeing extra bases all the way, he tore around first and then slid into second base in a cloud of glory.

"Where do you think you're going?" asked his teammate, who was also occupying second base.

Babe looked up at him and said, "Back to first if I can get there."

Stories like these just naturally seem to congregrate around Herman. It was not true, however, as John Lardner pointed out in his famous magazine piece on the Babe, that Herman tripled into a triple play; "but he once doubled into a double play, which is the next best thing."

That timeless deed occurred when Babe was playing for the Daffiness Boys, the Brooklyn Dodgers of the late twenties and thirties. With the bases full, Herman hit a line shot against the wall. The man on third scored easily but Dazzy Vance, who was on second, held up, thinking the ball might be caught. He reached third just ahead of the other baserunner, Chick Fewster, who had stopped midway between second and third and was scrambling back to the open bag.

Enter the Babe. Head down, arms pumping, running like a frightened ostrich, Herman charged past Fewster, who was so flustered at his appearance that he stepped off the base and was tagged out. By passing his teammate on the base paths, Babe became an automatic out, but his all-out charge did not cease until he landed on third base with the astonished Dazzy Vance. His day's work done, the Babe tipped his hat to the crowd and left the game.

Bird Song

"This is a town," Joe Falls, the columnist, wrote, "that has developed a true passion for a boy's game and a love-hate relationship for the men who play it." Falls was speaking of Detroit, and for one all-too-brief season, the city had a rapturous, wildly passionate love affair with Mark Fidrych, a twenty-one-year-old right-handed pitcher who went by the name of "the Bird." In those dark, pre–Sparky Anderson days, the Bird galvanized fans in Detroit, indeed all throughout the league. "He's the most exciting thing I've seen in any city I've been in," said Rusty Staub in 1976, the Bird's one great year. "I've never seen a city turn on like this. I've never seen anybody electrify the fans like this." "Electric" was the word most commonly used to describe Fidrych. And they still talk of him on the streets of Detroit and elsewhere.

For all the fanfare he would receive later on, the Bird was a nobody when he came to Tiger training camp in the spring of that year. He was a nonroster player summoned to pitch batting practice. His entire wardrobe consisted of some scruffy blue jeans and T-shirts, and a raggedy pair of tennis shoes. He looked like a refugee hippie. And no one expected him to stay around very long. With less than two years in the minors behind him, it was thought he'd need more seasoning before he'd be able to get major league hitters out. But after a negotiating dispute caused all rostered players to be locked out from training camp, the Tiger coaching staff gave Fidrych a longer look. And they looked and they looked and they still didn't believe what they saw.

The Bird, wrote Jerry Green, had "flamingo legs, a sparrow's countenance, and Harpo Marx plumage." Outgoing and effusive by nature, he showed his emotions freely when he pitched. He talked to anything and everybody—the fans, his infielders, his teammates in the dugout, the opposing players, the ball. Yes, the ball.

Fidrych talked to the baseball the way some people talk to plants. He caressed and soothed and encouraged it, and if need be, he cajoled and needled it. He said things like, "Great pitch, guy. Way to flow, you're in the groove now. Go for it!" and: "Flow, flow, you gotta flow now. You're doing it now. Come on, keep it moving, keep it going. Keep down, keep down. Fly now, fly!"

These conversations, in which the ball's response is not recorded, must've had some effect, because Fidrych made the roster to go up north with the Tigers. "The biggest rush of my life," he said about the day he learned he'd made the team. He was so excited, he couldn't stand up. His legs were momentarily paralyzed. After getting his legs functioning again, he then scrounged up the change and called his parents in Massachusetts.

In addition to his habit of talking to the ball, the Bird had other traits not in keeping with the cooler-than-thou demeanor so much in vogue among modern players. After making a good pitch he flapped his arms and shrieked like a prehistoric flying thing. "You're a bird, a goddamn bird," said a minor league coach who saw him do this, and the name stuck. The Bird was anything but cool. He ran full-speed out to the bullpen to take his warm-up throws. One time he got out there and realized he'd forgotten to put his cup on. "Oh well," he said, and dropped his drawers and stuck his cup in place, in full view of the people in the stands.

It's very possible Fidrych didn't know he was doing anything wrong. He had a naive, buoyant enthusiasm that wasn't forced or artificial. He played the game with joy. In a game in spring training, after picking Lou Brock off first base, the Bird cried out ecstatically, "I did it! I did it! I got him! I picked the great Lou Brock off first base!" Seeing Fidrych erupt, Brock, a man worthy of respect, said, "What'd you say, Mark?" To which Mark, quieting down immediately, said, "Uh, nothing, sir."

At the start of the '76 season, the Bird was a mop-up man, relegated to the pen. Only in May, with the Tiger pitching corps in shambles, did he get his first start. He pitched a two-hitter against the Indians that game, and after the final out he jumped into the arms of his catcher like he had just won the last game of the World Series. Then he went around to all his teammates and shook their hands. After that he sought out the groundskeepers and shook *their* hands too.

From there, the Bird took wing. He won nine of his first ten games and started the All-Star Game. In the process he charged up Tiger fans like no hometowner they had ever seen. *"We want the Bird! We want the Bird!"* they chanted in unison well after one of his games was over. And they wouldn't stop chanting until Mark, in his stocking feet, returned to the field to tell them to go home. Of the crowd's cheers, Fidrych said, "It gives my body a rush"—a feeling the fans shared. Watching him pitch was a rush.

For anyone who thought that the big leagues had become altogether too serious and grim-lipped, too stodgy and plain, the Bird was the perfect antidote. He waved his cap over his head and blew kisses to the crowd. He flapped his arms like wings and did double knee bends after each pitch. Before his half of the inning he would get down on his hands and knees and pat down the dirt mound to make it smooth and bump-free the way he liked. After a game he usually downed a glass of milk, followed by four or five beers. He deliberately dirtied his uniform with tobacco juice so his fellow Tigers would know he was one of them, a man who chewed.

But Bird's ongoing dialectic with his Spaldings was surely what energized the fans more than anything. The people loved it, and pretty soon ballplayers around the league started picking up on it. "I talked to the ball in Spanish," said the Cuban-born left-hander Mike Cuellar, "but I found out it was an American ball." Graig Nettles, then of the Yankees, told an interviewer what it was like facing Fidrych the first time. "It was on national TV," Nettles remembered. "It was funny because he was out there talking to the ball, so just when he started to wind up for his first pitch, I stepped out of the batter's box, and started talking to my bat. I said, 'Now, don't you listen to that ball . . .'" Apparently it did not, for Nettles got two hits off the Bird that day.

In one sense, however much of a phenomenon the Bird became, there's nothing new about his story. He is just another in a long line of pitchers, going back through Herb Score and beyond, to the great Smokey Joe Wood, who blew their arms out when young and ruined what could have been Hall of Fame careers. In 1977, after that glorious rookie season, it all began to fall apart for Fidrych. He tore cartilage in his knee in the spring, then developed a tendinitis condition in his right shoulder that put him out for the year. The pain cropped up again after two starts the next year, and he went onto the disabled list. Returning to the minors to pitch himself back into shape, everything seemed to be going well. He was scheduled to make a triumphant return to Tiger Stadium when the pain flared up anew, and forced him to call it off. Said Dave Rozema, a close friend of Fidrych's on the Tigers, "It just seems like, God . . . it's off and on. He's healthy, and something [bad] comes up. He's healthy, and something comes up again."

Fidrych kept trying, and he did eventually make it back to the majors for a few halting appearances. But the pop in his fastball was gone, and he was washed up at twenty-six. Bird's song had turned sad.

"I guess the saddest things I've ever seen in baseball are the guys that are cut down in mid-career by freak accidents and injuries. You may not know them personally, but as an athlete you can identify with them," said Al Kaline, who played right field for so many years in Detroit. "The whole team, even the other teams, are all pulling for Fidrych to make it, because he's a tremendous guy and he loves playing baseball. But what he's gone through in the last four years is tragic. And a real loss for baseball, too. The Bird just electrified the fans. It's hard to explain, but everyone in the stands was just so happy and emotional when he pitched. But all the poor kid had was just that one great season."

It's tempting to leave Bird's story at that: to see him as a boy, like Icarus, who had one short go at glory and blew it, a kind of golden failure. But Fidrych, who now lives in Massachusetts and works as a landscape gardener and part-time actor, doesn't see himself that way. "I look at what I had before and what I have now," he has said, "and now is a lot better." Furthermore: "I never think about what might have been. I'm happy with what I achieved, and I think about what I got now. For me, that's plenty."

Even at his ball-talking height, Fidrych dismissed jokes about him being a flake. He was, in his eyes, just being himself, and that had nothing to do with the labels other people put on him. That was their problem, not his. And now, with his ballplaying days behind him, he's still being himself.

"When it's gone," he says in reflection, "all you can say is: It's gone, and this is what I got out of it.'"

Oil Can

Dennis "Oil Can" Boyd is an up-and-comer in flakedom, an argument against all those who claim there are no more genuine screwballs left in the game. Boyd, a pitcher for the Red Sox, stands six foot one and weighs a hundred and forty-five pounds, but claims he has a "two-hundred-pound fastball." In the tradition of Satchel Paige, who also had names for his various pitches, Boyd has a "back-door screwball," "a sinkin' sinker," and the "slippery slider." But Oil Can isn't about to show all he's got. "I want to go out of this game gray-headed," he says in a Mississippi drawl. "That's why I'm saving some of my pitches for my old age."

Boyd was tabbed as a hotdogger on his very first day in the big leagues. On Opening Day against the Yankees, first baseman Bill Buckner made a diving stop of a hard-hit ground ball down the line, and the scrawny right-hander ran over from the mound and shook his hand. Later in the season, he pumped his fist in celebration after striking out an A's hitter in a tight situation—a gesture the A's team thought was intended to show their man up. In fact, many around the league do not appreciate the Can's showboating tendencies and want to make him look bad. Boyd wonders why. "We always played with a little hotdogging growing up because that was the only way we knew how because we were having so much fun," he says. "I've been that way since I was knee-high to a snake."

Boyd's colloquialisms stem from his upbringing in Meridien, Mississippi, where he got his nickname. It seems "oil" was the word for beer in the local argot, and Oil Can, who's been drinking almost as long as he's been throwing his backdoor screwball, could toss down six-packs like he had a hole in his shoe. He is one of those rare individuals who can drink and eat and eat and drink and not ever gain a pound. His father, Willie James Boyd, who played for the Homestead Grays in black ball, didn't mind the drinking as long as his son stayed out of trouble. And Dennis stayed out of trouble because he spent all his time down at the ballyard.

Now he's moved up to the big show, but his taste for beer—and lots of it—remains strong as ever. "It wasn't nothing for me [as a teenager] to drink a six-pack and go out and play a game of baseball," he told Murray Chass. "Now I don't do that no more. I wait until after the game to drink a six-pack."

The Motivator

Where would baseball be without men like Rocky Bridges, tobacco-chewing coach of the San Francisco Giants?

While managing in the minors, Bridges sprinted out onto the field, circled the pitcher's mound twice, and then ran back to the dugout without saying a word to anyone.

After his team played an exhibition with a touring Japanese squad, he said, "An hour after the game you want to go out and play them again."

For one of those ridiculous promotional stunts that baseball P.R. men dream up to boost the gate, Bridges entered a pregame cow-milking contest and finished second. Said he: "I didn't try too hard. I was afraid I'd get emotionally involved with the cow."

Plagued by a weight problem, Rocky experimented with a new diet drink of his own making: "You mix two jiggers of Scotch to one jigger of Metrecal. So far I've lost five pounds and my driver's license."

Then there is the inspirational side of Bridges. On the first day of spring training one year, readying to start a new season, he gathered his Phoenix Giants team around him in a circle on the grass. His purpose was to motivate them for the coming months ahead—to give them one piece of wisdom, the benefit of all his years in baseball, that they could take with them through the long, hard minor league season and perhaps even fall back on during those moments of doubt and introspection that every ballplayer, at every level of the game, must face.

"Men, I'm just going to say one thing to you," Rocky Bridges told his players, holding the thumb and forefinger of his right hand an inch apart. "I just want you all to remember that you're only this far away from big league pussy."

Honorable Mentions

To celebrate his one hundredth career homer, Jimmy Piersall ran the bases backward.

When Germany Schaefer hit a home run after predicting to his teammates that he would, he slid into first, slid into second, slid into third and, to complete his dirty sweep of the bases, slid home.

Tiger pitcher Bill Faul once ate a live toad and bit the head off a parakeet.

Joe Charbonneau of the Indians used to pop the caps off beer bottles with his teeth.

José Cardenal, wrote Mike Royko, "could hardly play at

all during one spring training because he said his eyelid was stuck shut. The next year, he couldn't play in spring training because a cricket in his motel room kept him awake all night." For those times when his hair needed sprucing up, José also used to hide his Afro comb in the ivy along the walls at Wrigley Field.

In 1971 Dock Ellis, a pitcher for the Pirates, appeared on the dugout steps in hair curlers, a first in baseball annals.

The Red Sox's Bernie Carbo could not go on a road trip without bringing along his pet stuffed gorilla.

Doug Rader told a kid that if he wanted to grow up to be a big leaguer, he had to eat Willie McCovey bubble gum cards. While in the majors Rader regularly ate breakfast at hotel restaurants with shaving cream plastered over his face.

Whirlybird Walk, a pitcher, went up to hit without a bat and walked to the mound without a glove.

Mark Lemongello of the Astros left teeth marks in his shoulder after biting himself during a fit of temper.

Don Cardwell and Dick Farrell stuck dead fish in Satchel Paige's shoes and hammered his uniform to the ceiling when the three were on a Philadelphia farm club in the fifties.

Randy Jones, according to Roy Blount, Jr., "used to go to a women's beauty parlor to get his hair done—would sit there wearing pink plastic curlers and dipping snuff."

Blount also says that Jackie Price was known to play catch while standing on his head and Ross "Evil Eyes" Grimsley, formerly of the Orioles, was cured of a pitching slump by a witch's charm.

One season in the late forties Cleveland fan Charlie Lupica climbed atop a flagpole and vowed not to come down until his team passed the Yankees in the standings. He came down one hundred and seventeen days later.

In a contest, Braves owner Ted Turner rolled a baseball from home to first with his nose.

Before the practice was banned, Mel Hall of the Indians used to stuff his batting gloves halfway into his back pocket. The gloves flapped when he ran, as he said, "waving good-bye" to everyone.

Coaches and managers waved at Jackie Brandt in the outfield, trying to get him to adjust his position according to the batter at the plate. Happy to oblige, Jackie jumped up and down frantically for a minute, then stayed exactly where he was.

Asked the distance between home plate and second base, Billy Gleason of the St. Louis Browns said, "I don't know. I never ran that way."

Bill Lee, the Red Sox pitcher, used to sprinkle marijuana on his cornflakes in the morning.

Steve Dalkowski and a teammate once drilled holes in the wall of their hotel suite to watch a Miss Universe pageant contestant get dressed in the next room.

Kirby Higbe, Brooklyn Dodger pitcher and unreconstructed ladies' man, wired home to his wife as the team neared the end of a road trip: "Arriving April 1. Meet me on the dock if you want to be the first. Kirby."

9
Scrapbook for the Eighties: Pieces and Things, Designed to Amuse

"Baseball is just about the best thing this country has going for it."

—PETE ROSE

Lifestyles of the Rich and Famous

1
LITERACY IN BASEBALL

"I THINK most ballplayers read the sports pages, but I'm sorry to say that in most cases that's all they read," said the erudite Brewers catcher Ted Simmons, who could've been referring to the somewhat less erudite second baseman for the Dodgers, Steve Sax.

One day Sax noticed his manager Tommy Lasorda reading the *Wall Street Journal* on the team bus.

"Hey," Sax said, "lemme borrow the sports section, would ya?"

2
CITIZENSHIP

The scene opens in Florida. It's springtime, and the exhibition season is under way. Mike Wolf, a White Sox infielder, is standing outside his team's hotel when he sees a man grab a woman's purse and take off running down the street.

Upon hearing the woman's cries of alarm, Wolf flies off in pursuit of the thief.

Then stops.

"I started chasing him," says Wolf later, "and then I asked myself, 'What am I going to do if I catch him?'"

3
SHARING THE WEALTH

When Pete Rose was playing for the Phillies, he put together a twenty-three-game hitting streak, the longest in the majors that year. This won him a twenty-three-thousand-dollar cash prize, a grand for each game.

But Pete did not keep the money for himself; he divided it among the Phillie coaches, trainers and clubhouse people. The reason?

Said Pete, "They've helped me tremendously. I'm one who likes to do something for the little guys, and not just the superstars. Besides, it's a good tax write-off."

A Short History of the Hair-Dryer in the Major Leagues

Joe Pepitone was the first ballplayer to use a hair-dryer in a major league locker room. This occurred in the early sixties when Joe, a dandy if there ever was one, was playing first base for the Yankees in the declining years of their dynasty. Pepi thought his innovation would get him into the Hall of Fame. He was wrong. It did, however, begin a tonsorial revolution in professional baseball.

After his breakthrough the practice of using hair-dryers spread around the majors, except to Derrel Thomas, who, according to Jay Johnstone, "dried his hair in a microwave oven." Electrical outlets for blow-dryers have become standard locker-room equipment for stadiums. And Bob Lemon notes that they are now an essential part of the daily grooming habits of the modern ballplayer.

"Today's players like to play their stereos early," he says, "because after the game their hair-dryers cause static."

Have Ego, Will Travel

When Bobby Bonds broke into the majors, some touted him as the next Willie Mays. Before he was through he almost became the next Bobo Newsom. Landing with the Cubs after being traded six times in the previous six years, Bobby said, "I would like to find a home in baseball. The only thing I've been a part of the last six years is American Airlines."

One year Bonds was hired to participate in a batting experiment designed to test a new, livelier "rabbit" baseball. Stepping into the cage, he hit six or seven soaring, prodigious homers in about as many swings, the balls all flying well over the four-hundred-foot marker.

Observing this feat was a man from the commissioner's office who pronounced the experiment a failure. The ball was much too lively ever to use in a real game, he said.

Bonds disagreed. "Sir," he said, "I see no difference in the ball at all. I just had a good day."

A Survivor Speaks

They say Reggie Jackson has a stone glove. They called Greg Luzinski a butcher in the outfield. But what about Carlos Lopez?

In one calamity-filled week Lopez collided with two of his Baltimore Oriole teammates, knocking them both out of the game and onto the disabled list. Asked what he thought of Lopez's outfielding abilities, O's right fielder Ken Singleton said, "He'll never take me alive."

The Texas Strangers

Will the Texas Rangers never come around? Other teams go up and down, but the Rangers always seem to be down.

The story of the franchise, says Peter Gammons, "reads like the history of a depressed banana republic."

After being named general manager of the club, Joe Klein's first piece of fan mail was a postcard with one word printed on the back: CONDOLENCES.

When Don Zimmer was manager, he went on a diet. A Texas radio station suggested that the best way for him to lose weight was to eat only on the days the Rangers won.

Asked if she'd ever seen a major league team play, a woman trying out to be a batgirl for the Texas A & M baseball team said, "No, but I've seen the Texas Rangers play several times."

Sizing up the team's hitters a few years ago, batting coach Merv Rettenmund said, "I don't want to knock our offensive firepower, but to save time the ground crew could drag the infield during batting practice."

Asked if his presence would pull the team out of its customary place in the second division, Cliff Johnson said, "My name's Cliff, not Moses."

At the start of one season reporter Randy Galloway did a rip-and-slash piece on the Strangers, as they are known in Texas, after they lost seven of their first ten games. Bump Wills, the team's shortstop, was so incensed that he taped the article to his locker with the note: "Wait till July." When July came around and the team fell into another long losing streak, Wills called Galloway over to his locker.

"You're right," he said, ripping the story into shreds. "We stink."

Ballplayer as Confused Individual

"I'm a baseball player when I have the uniform on. But otherwise I'm your basic confused human being," said pitcher John Curtis, who must've been out of his uniform when he made this comment, because to us most ballplayers seem a little like Roy Smalley.

Asked why he always hit so well in Seattle's Kingdome, Smalley said, "It's not because the Mariners have a bad pitching staff, because they don't. It's not because I see the ball well here, because I don't. It's not because I'm swinging great, because I'm not. You figure it out."

If Roy sounds a tad confused, think of how his uncle Gene Mauch, who used to manage him on the Twins, felt. "Sometimes I look on Roy as my nephew," he said at the time, "but sometimes only as my sister's son."

You figure it out.

Short Story

The onetime Dodger infield of Steve Garvey, Davey Lopes, Bill Russell and Ron Cey were good, but they were also short.

One year they were all invited to a banquet in Los Angeles in their honor, but not one of the four showed up.

Writer Lyle Spencer had a reason why they couldn't make it: "They're out at Dodger Stadium doing their stretching exercises, trying to get up to five foot seven."

Great Excuses Department

Claudell Washington was traded in mid-season from the Rangers to the White Sox but failed to report to his new team for four days.

"I overslept," explained Claudell.

Ump Humor

One time Billy Martin, managing the A's, asked ump Bill Kunkel to smell one of Gaylord Perry's baseballs for any possible doctoring.

"I can't," Kunkel told him. "I have allergies and a deviated septum."

"Christ," said Martin. "I got an umpire who can't see or smell."

*   *   *

Called out on a pitch that in his view was well outside, Rick Monday flipped his bat in disgust to the startled ump behind the plate. "Here," he said, "you hit that pitch. I can't."

After which Monday was tossed.

*   *   *

Scott Ostler of the *Los Angeles Times:* "Have you looked at some of the umpires lately? Judging from their waistlines, throwing Earl Weaver out of games is the only exercise they get."

*   *   *

Earl Weaver, to an ump (and resurrecting an old line): "You fool! You idiot! You could show up on *What's My Line?* wearing a mask and a chest protector, and still nobody'd mistake you for an umpire!"

*   *   *

Padres manager Dick Williams, calling out to one of his players as he approached an ump: "Get the hell away from him! Don't you know his pet rat died this morning?"

*   *   *

Billy Martin, managing the Yankees, rushed onto the field to dispute a call.

"Dammit, Billy," said the ump, Al Clark. "I saw the play and I called it right. Now what the hell are you doing here?"

"Gee, Al," Billy said in a mock-hurt voice. "I was just coming out here to ask you the same thing."

*   *   *

In that famous Fourth of July Braves-Mets game in 1985 that went nineteen innings and lasted until almost four in the morning, ump Terry Tata ejected Darryl Strawberry in the seventeenth for heatedly arguing a called third strike.

Explaining to the Mets right fielder why he called the pitch the way he did, Tata said, "The strike zone changes at three A.M."

*   *   *

Mark Belanger became incensed after ump Russ Goetz called a runner safe at second who Belanger contended was out. But Goetz didn't toss the Orioles shortstop—and this only infuriated him more.

After the game Belanger launched into another tirade against the ump, saying, "How could he be doing his job when he didn't throw me out after all the things I called him?"

Another Ump Story

Before becoming a media heavy, Ron Luciano was an umpire heavy who, according to William Furlong, "looked like nothing so much as an elephant doing an *entrechat-dix*" when he made one of his balletic out calls. Luciano, said another observer, was the only person in the world who could make "Strike!" into a four-syllable word.

But Luciano's hammy reputation did not endear him to everyone. Besides Earl Weaver, there was Alex Johnson. Whenever Luciano was umping balls and strikes, the petulant Angels outfielder always followed the same ritual. He walked up to the plate, sniffed the air and, looking at Luciano, said, "What smells?"

Pitchers, on Their Pitches

Allen Ripley, the journeyman right-hander, called one of his pitches "an ecological fastball." "Because," he said, "it never traveled faster than fifty-five miles per hour."

Dan Quisenberry has names for two of his pitches:

The "At-Em" Ball: "That's the one I hope the guy will hit it at somebody," he explained.

The Titanic: "It's supposed to be unsinkable, but when it starts to go down, it can be a real disaster."

But Tug McGraw, recently retired, had the most colorful arsenal of deliveries. They were:

The Peggy Lee: "After they swung and missed, they said, 'Is that all there is?'"

The John Jameson: "Straight, the way I like my Irish whiskey."

The Cutty Sark: "It sailed."

The Bo Derek: "This one had a nice little tail on it."

The Frank Sinatra: "After they swung and connected, it was 'Fly me to the moon.'"

Art News

The Cincinnati Art Museum recently announced that the city's most famous citizen, Pete Rose, will have his portrait painted by internationally known artist Andy Warhol.

Rose's reaction: "I just put all my faith in War, Warhaw, Warhall? What is it? Oh, yeah, Warhol. I think he's a well-respected artist. Somebody told me he did Ali."

The Hit

As Pete Rose neared Ty Cobb's all-time hit mark, the pack of reporters following him around the clubhouse after each game got bigger and bigger.

At one point Rose asked them, "Why don't you guys all leave your numbers? When I get The Hit, I'll call you."

* * *

One reporter asked Rose if he thought Ty Cobb might be looking down on him from above when he broke the record.

"From what I know of Cobb, he might not be up there," Pete said.

* * *

In the thick of the hunt, *Cincinnati Enquirer* columnist Tim Sullivan sought out a St. Louis psychic who claimed to have recently spoken with Harry Truman. Sullivan hoped to speak to Cobb and hear what he had to say about the man about to surpass him in hits.

The psychic did apparently reach Cobb, who was asked if Rose was his equal as a ballplayer. "Yeah, 'cause he has my help," replied The Voice of Cobb. "He's good . . . I'm supposed to be a nice guy about this."

Cobb was then asked if he was bothered by Rose breaking the record.

"Not really," came the answer. "He wouldn't break it if I was still doing the work. He's great, but he's not that great."

* * *

In the spring of '85 Rose, as manager of the Reds, told a young pitcher named Ron Robinson that he was being sent to the minors for more seasoning. Rose, uncomfortable about having to break the bad news to the kid, asked him if he had anything he wanted to say.

"Yeah," Robinson said sharply. "I hope you don't get any more hits."

Flabbergasted, Rose asked the pitcher to repeat himself. He wasn't sure he heard right.

"I hope you stop hitting," the pitcher said. Then, in a softer voice, he added, "Because I don't want you to get The Hit until I get back to the majors."

(Robinson did make it back to the Reds in time to see The Hit.)

*   *   *

Pitcher Andy McGaffigan explains what it's like to play under a team managed by Pete Rose:

"This time of the year, when it's hot, everybody tends to start thinking about the winter. But Pete comes to the park ready to play every day.

"There are times when you think, 'Crap, it's hot and I'm tired.' Every time you think that, here's Pete Rose hitting a single and stretching it into a double. You say, 'Here's a guy who's forty-four years old. The problem is either with me or with him.'

"Then you go look at the record and say, 'It must be me.'"

*   *   *

In a press conference before the game of The Hit, somebody asked Rose if it would help if he knew what pitches were coming. Pete said that would only mess him up, and told the story of the game early in his career when Phillies Manager Gene Mauch ordered his catcher to let Rose know beforehand what each pitch would be.

The object was to screw Rose up—and it worked. Each time Rose came up the Phillies catcher, Mike Ryan, let him know what was coming—a curve or a fastball or whatever. Rose started thinking too much, and made three weak outs in three times up.

Then, in the ninth inning, Rose came up again. Ryan told him, "Curveball," but this time Rose ignored him completely. He got the fastball he was looking for and hit a home run off the top of the scoreboard to win the game for the Reds.

The next day Rose, the leadoff batter, greeted Ryan behind the plate. "Hey Mike," he said, "how ya doin'?"

And Ryan looked up and said, "Mauch told me to tell you to go to hell."

* * *

Mickey Mantle, on Pete Rose's all-time hit mark: "Hell, if I'd a hit that many singles, I'd a wore a dress."

The Arrowhead

Now that Dave Kingman has over four hundred career home runs, you might think the press and his fellow players would lighten up on him, give him some respect.

No way.

Says Reggie Jackson: "Hey, you can say I won't make the Hall of Fame. You can say I stink. But don't put me in the same story with that guy."

Adds Billy Martin: "Dave Kingman? He's an arrowhead."

And sportswriter Tom Boswell: "If Kingman ever gets into the Hall of Fame, the place should be quarantined."

Lefty and Johnny

In his prime Steve Carlton was, as Pete Rose said, "the best pitcher in the world, unless the Russians have got one I haven't seen." But one man had his number: Johnny Bench.

While hitters around the National League trembled before Carlton, Lefty himself fell to pieces whenever he had to face Bench, who hit him like a batting practice pitcher. Bench, among others, said it was uncanny how easily he could handle the three-time Cy Young winner. For some unfathomable reason he seemed to know the pitch ahead of time, before it ever left Carlton's hand.

Carlton was aware of Bench's mastery over him, and it rankled him no end. During the off-season one year, he was out hunting, a favorite pastime of his. Just past dawn, he was crouched behind a duck blind in a swampy area of the woods.

Some geese appeared overhead but Carlton, temporarily

distracted, didn't react quickly enough, and missed on every shot. The flock passed safely out of range and Carlton, angry with himself, stood there in sullen silence. A moment went by. Then he fired off a lone shot into the sky.

"There," he said. "That one's for Bench."

Lefty and Nolan

While Steve Carlton is considered a more complete pitcher, Nolan Ryan is known primarily as a man who can bring it. "He's baseball's exorcist," said one batter. "He scares the devil out of you." Said Reggie Smith after being whiffed on three pitches by Ryan: "If I'm going to be struck out, that's the way to go. It may sound strange, but I actually enjoyed that. It was like a surgeon's knife—quick and painless." Ryan and Goose Gossage have thrown the fastest fastballs ever recorded on the JUGS gun: one hundred three miles per hour.

Yet, for all their pitching skills, the race by Carlton and Ryan to eclipse Walter Johnson's longtime career K mark and then to break the four-thousand barrier received relatively little public attention. Certainly nothing to compare to the media feast enjoyed by Pete Rose as he tracked Ty Cobb. So why no daily newspaper strikeout counts, why no national magazine covers, why so little public fuss?

Newspaper columnist Wayne Parrish asked Ryan about it and the big Texan answered, "If you had Reggie Jackson and Pete Rose going after the same hit record, it would make great print. But Carlton doesn't talk at all and I really have nothing to say about it."

Oh.

Lefty and Tim

First with St. Louis, then with the Phillies, Lefty Carlton's principal batterymate for many years was Tim McCarver, now a broadcaster. The two men were close on and off the field. Indeed, on the days Carlton pitched, he requested McCarver to be the catcher.

Said Tim, "When I die, they're going to bury me in the cemetery sixty feet six inches from Lefty."

How to Be Traded in One Easy Lesson

Dave Heaverlo, the pitcher, explains how he finally got Oakland to trade him:

"I tried growing a beard. That didn't work. I became the player rep. That didn't work. Then I bought a house. That worked."

Two Swingers

Don Mattingly of the Yankee has a swing, remarked Phil Elderkin, that "belongs in the Louvre."

Tim Foli, the veteran shortstop, has a pretty swing too. "Tim has one of the most beautiful home run cuts in baseball," said a former batting coach. "The only problem is, the ball doesn't go far enough."

Chutzpah

1

Though he'd only played in the minors, catcher Bill Nahorodny refused to sign a contract with the Phils, holding out for more money.

"There's no reason to squabble. I've done it all," said Nahorodny. "It's not my fault that it hasn't been done in the major leagues."

2

Reliever Buddy Schultz of the Cardinals was sent down to the minors after developing arm trouble. Schultz resented the team's action, saying, "I'm better than any left-hander they've got. The only question is whether I can throw."

Big Moments for Ordinary Guys

Asked what he was thinking as he rounded the bases after a game-winning home run, Jim Hickman said, "As usual—nothing."

Cincy catcher Dave Van Gorder hit his first-ever major league home run against the Phillies. His thoughts? "I thought as I got to second, 'Did I touch first?'"

Utility man Stan Papi, after hitting a homer, a triple and a single to help win a game for the Tigers: "I've never had a crowd in the big leagues even clap for me before. On Opening Day when I was with Boston, I got a standing boo."

A Word from Jerry

In his one-year stint as Padres manager, Jerry Coleman explained how he got along so well with his players:

"A guy who's basically a good, hard-nosed player, having a good year, if I catch him out at four A.M. with a broad, I'd tend to look the other way."

The Cobra

You don't hear so much about Dave Parker these days. Oh, he's still around, having been granted a second life on the Reds, but he's not the same cocky, big-talking guy we remember from his days as a Pirate. In those heady days, as Larry Sloman said, Parker didn't merely want a candy bar named after him—he wanted an entire flavor.

On a Pittsburgh Pirate team filled with loud, boisterous and handsomely talented men, Parker was the loudest and most talented of all. Asked why he wore a Star of David around his neck, he replied, "Because I'm David and I'm a star."

A poll of National League general managers rated him the best all-around player in the game. "Basically," he said, assessing the results, "I think they're right." When Phil Garner started ragging on him for showing up late to Pirate training camp one year, Parker told him, "If I hit like you do, I'd have been here since Christmas!"

As with Reggie Jackson, Parker's swagger irritated some and delighted others. He called Greg Luzinski, another outfielder of impressive bulk, "a pig." The remark caused a stir and big Dave backed off, claiming he had been misquoted. "I didn't call him that," he corrected. "I called him a rhino."

After he and Willie Stargell led the Pirates to the World Championship, Parker fell off the mountain. Injuries and other problems plagued the Cobra, and he gained weight. His estimated salary a few years ago was a million-plus a season. "Although a lot is deferred income," *Sport* magazine commented, "it still looks like he's paid by the pound." Told that Parker had become a vegetarian, John Candelaria, a former teammate, said, "What does he eat, palm trees? Redwoods?"

But the trouble-plagued star got in a parting shot of his own. At the end of one season, expecting to be traded over the winter, Parker hoisted a glass of wine in the Pirate club-house and, smiling, gave this toast to his teammates:

> "Here's to all the Buccos,
> May we never, ever disagree.
> But in case we do,
> The hell with all of you,
> And here's to me!"

The Way They Were

Before coming to the Angels, Rod Carew labored in Minnesota under the tight-fisted Twins owner Calvin Griffith. Griffith, who's since sold the team, had the instincts of a spinster and the tact of a dragon.

Come salary time one year, Griffith was in a hard bargaining session with Rod Carew's agent, who was negotiating for a big raise for his client.

Griffith didn't think he deserved it. "All Carew ever does is hit singles," he said scornfully.

"Yeah, I know," his agent said. "But every time up?"

Jim and Joe

Before a recent All-Star Game Joe DiMaggio was standing around the batting cage watching the American Leaguers take their practice swings. When Jim Rice came up, DiMaggio moved a few steps closer and concentrated on the hitter.

"Jim," he said, as line drive after line drive sprang off Rice's bat, "you make the ball look so lively."

"Just trying to hit it somewhere, Joe," said Rice, who kept swinging away.

Run That by Me Again, Would Ya?

Late in a close game in the seventies, Paul Molitor came up to face Sparky Lyle, on the mound for the Yankees. It was a crucial moment in a game the Yankees badly needed to win, and Lyle, who'd never pitched against the Brewers second baseman, looked like he needed help.

Jogging over from third to offer advice was Graig Nettles. "Watch out for this guy. He likes to bunt," Nettles told Sparky, who thanked him for the tip and settled down to pitch.

With Nettles sneaking in on the grass, Lyle threw a slider and Molitor swung for everything he was worth, hitting the first pitch far over the left field wall for a home run.

As Molitor rounded the bases, Nettles went back over to console Lyle, who looked even more puzzled than before.

"He does bunt, you know," Nettles told him. "But you've got to throw him more than one pitch."

George Stories

1

After the Yankees got off to a bad start one season, George began flying in to meet the team wherever it played on road trips. Alone among his teammates, Graig Nettles welcomed George's presence.

"The more we lose, the more he'll fly in, right?" Nettles reasoned. "And the more he flies, the better his chances are that his plane will crash."

2

One time a huge, three-hundred-fifty-pound man waddled past the Yankee team bus and Graig Nettles called out

from an open window, "Hey George, hurry up and get
aboard or we'll have to leave without you!"

3

"I'm hard on people. I know that," said George, who is
especially hard on baseball managers. He fires them like
some people change their socks.

After a dismal Yankee loss to the Red Sox a few years
ago, George demanded that a hotel phone operator be fired
after she refused to place a long distance call for him from
the lobby bar.

Said then–Yankee manager Dick Howser: "At least the
day wasn't a total loss. George had somebody fired."

4

Sparky Lyle, the ex-Yankee, wrote in his book that
George once fired an employee over a tuna fish sandwich.

Responded George: "It's an outright lie that I fired an
office girl over a tuna fish sandwich. I'm almost certain it was
peanut butter and jelly."

5

Like any good tyrant, George loves edicts. One edict he
passed was against long hair. Lou Piniella protested this
rule, saying that if Jesus Christ had long hair, why couldn't
ballplayers?

George asked Lou to step over to a window in George's
office. "Do you see that soccer stadium out in the distance?"
he said, pointing.

"Yes sir," said Lou.

"And do you notice that pool beside it?" asked George.
"Yes."

"Well, Lou," said George. "The day you can go over

there and walk across that pool, you can wear your hair any way you want."

6

"It's like Shakespeare," said Bob Lemon, one of the many managers hired and fired by George. "He writes the plays and we act them out."

One of George's most celebrated performances was one in which he played both actor and writer. After the Yankees lost the World Series to the Dodgers, George broke his hand (he claimed) in a fight with two Dodger fans in a Los Angeles hotel. Since the fight took place in an elevator, and the two Dodger fans never came forward, many people did not believe George's version of events.

Not Reggie Jackson, however. He said he believed George: "He probably did punch out two Dodger fans, as long as they were ages nine and ten."

10
Aches and Pains No More

"The trick is to grow up without growing old."
—CASEY STENGEL

LUKE APPLING'S NICKNAME was "Old Aches and Pains." They called him that because he was a minor hypochondriac, always complaining about ailments of one kind or another. "When Appling was around," Maury Allen wrote, "the real blunder was to ask him, 'How do you feel?' It would sometimes take half an hour before he stopped telling you."

In retrospect, he may have had good reason to complain. Here was a future Hall of Famer, a man voted the best White Sox player of all time, and his teammates were a bunch of boobs. Beginning in 1930, Appling played two decades for a club that never once seriously threatened for the title, and ordinarily finished in the second division. Said baseball historian David Nemec: "No other player in the game's history would play for so long with a club that was never once in contention." No wonder Appling was in such pain.

Then as now, the city of Chicago was divided between two teams; the Sox represented the South Side and the Cubs had the North. Despite their reputation as legendary losers, the Cubs actually fielded some pretty good teams in the thirties and forties—a claim their crosstown rivals could not make. Jean Shepherd, the humorist, explains what it was like to follow the White Sox: "Being a White Sox fan meant measuring victory in terms of defeat. A 6–5 defeat was a good day. A big rally was Wally Moses doubling down the right field line." In this sea of incompetence one man, almost by himself, stood against the tide. Again, Jean Shepherd: "Luke Appling led the league with a .388 average one year and knocked in about twenty-seven runs. There were no men on base. It was like he was the only human being alive in a jungle full of tigers, trying to keep the human race alive."

Appling was one of those select players who flourished into middle age. At forty-two, in his next to last season, he hit over .300 while playing a full schedule of games for the sixth-place Chisox. It was a solid, workmanlike performance in a career known for its steadiness and dependability. You could not count on much with the White Sox in those days, but you could go to the bank on Appling rapping out his one hundred sixty-five hits or so, and fielding his position as cleanly as any in the game.

Twice he won the American League batting championship. Like Brett or Carew, he usually got good wood on the ball, seldom striking out. He had a good, sharp eye and the bat control of a master. He fouled off pitches seemingly at will. Pitchers worked him to a two-strike count, then had to throw him eight or ten or twelve pitches or more as Appling kept fouling off pitches until, like a gourmand selecting from the hors d'oeuvre tray, he found something he liked. One year, the story goes, the White Sox management turned down his request for some free baseballs. An irked Appling got revenge by purposely fouling off dozens of baseballs into the stands during batting practice. In a similar incident he deliberately fouled off a number of balls into the stands in D.C. when the Senators wouldn't give him free passes for some old friends visiting from High Point, North Carolina, his hometown. And Dizzy Trout got so mad at Luke for fouling off his pitches that he threw his glove at him.

In 1950, after years and years of trying to keep the human race alive, Old Aches and Pains let someone else take on the burden. His uniform—No. 4—was retired, the first White Sox player to be so honored. He went on to coach in the majors and in 1967, three years after being named to the Hall of Fame, he became manager of the Kansas City A's. But he lasted little more than a month in the job as the A's, a throwback to his old White Sox teams, lost thirty of their first forty games. As baseball analyst Guy Waterman points out, Appling is one of the few managers in major league history with a winning percentage lower than his lifetime batting average.

This little statistical indignity, a footnote to a great career, might have been Appling's final resting place in baseball lore. Like so many other onetime greats, he had shrunk to the size of an answer in a trivia quiz. But there was more to come, more for Appling to do. One more moment, another big at bat. And, though perhaps he did not realize it during all those years of laboring with the hapless White Sox, and then after retirement, when he was managing in the minors and teaching young men how to hit, Luke had been waiting all his life for it.

By his own admission, the biggest thrill of Lucius Benjamin Appling's life came three decades after he retired, in 1981, when he hit a looping home run off fellow Hall of Famer Warren Spahn in the first inning of the first-ever Cracker Jack Old-Timers Classic in RFK Stadium in Washington, D.C. That one swing garnered him more attention than he received in two decades on the White Sox, propelling his round, chubby figure onto the national news shows. The news-wire photograph of him swinging, his chipmunk cheek clearly bulging with chaw, made the front pages of sports sections around the country. Fan reaction was sudden and strong. "I've got arthritis in two fingers from signing autographs," he joked, and letters were still coming into him months after the game. Dubbed "Home Run" Appling, he was accorded the star treatment on the banquet circuit the following winter. He was seventy-five years old at the time.

But Luke almost didn't get his shot at glory. The game had to be delayed an hour that evening and was in danger of being called after a sudden July thunderstorm hit the capital, leaving the grass field at RFK Stadium wet and slippery and dotted with small puddles. Stan Musial stood in the middle of a squall telling a live TV news remote that yes, the game would go on, the old-timers were determined to play no matter what, and the people should keep coming out to the park, they'd see a great show after all. The fans listened to Stan—when had he ever let them down?—and in time the rains quit, just like he said they would. Some twenty-nine thousand people put up with the discomfort and foul weather to be on hand, not a bad gate for a meaningless exhibition played by middle-aged men and older. "The Ben-Gay Bowl," someone called it.

Some analysts said the organizers of the Cracker Jack had a political motive: If D.C. fans came out in big numbers, they would be arguing with their feet for the return of major league baseball to an area that had been bereft for a decade. But, in all likelihood, even in politics-mad Washington the fans had no hidden agenda. They were there for the game, and the memories.

You can't get away from sentiment in old-timers games because that's what they're all about. We want to see these old guys play because the last time we saw them, they were young and so were we. They were the companions of our youth. With them we hope to recover a piece of ourselves, a piece of our past that has been buried. We're curious, we want to know (though already sensing the answer): Has time beaten down on these great players as it has ourselves? That it has, of course, saddens and disturbs us, but seen in another light this knowledge provides great joy. Thomas Boswell writes, "We are moved by these old heroes partly because of our soft sorrow at seeing them grow older, but it's just as true that we are pleased to see them, at last, in proper human proportion. Once, perhaps, we wanted them to be myths but, before we say goodbye, we'd like to see them simply as our fellow men." After the game the old-timers from both sides, the American and National, came onto the field and applauded the fans, as if in recognition of their shared destiny.

Organized in order to gain publicity for its principal sponsor, the Cracker Jack was a benefit for the Professional Ballplayers of America, a group that assists retired players, particularly ones who left the game before the establishment of the pension plan. While most old-timers games take place before a regular season contest, the Washington D.C. Cracker Jack was neither a sideshow nor a preliminary; it was the main event. Fans came to see the old-timers play, that's all.

This fact largely explains why so many prominent names showed up for the event. Each side fielded close to a dream team of ex- (and still extant) ballplayers. The American roster featured Whitey Ford, Bob Feller, Enos Slaughter, Harmon Killebrew, Johnny Mize, Bobby Richardson and Brooks Robinson; the potent National League card included Stan Musial, Willie Mays, Henry Aaron, Willie McCovey, Lou Brock, Bill Mazeroski, Ernie Banks, Robin Roberts, Dick Groat and Hoyt Wilhelm. Pee Wee Reese and Red Schoendienst started at short and second for the Nationals, and the opposing battery was Bill Freehan at catcher and Early Wynn on the mound. The managers were Al Lopez and Walter Alston; up in the booth was Red Barber. Lou Brock, who, at forty-two, was one of the youngest men on the field, said he was thrilled to play in a game with so many of his heroes.

These men were, of course, far from their prime. Middle-aged or older, they were badly out of shape, some as fat as house cats. "A few of them couldn't hit a ball to the outfield with a fungo bat," remarked Denis Collins of the *Washington Post*. "Most couldn't make first string on a decent high school team." Richie Ashburn warned that they'd better keep plenty of ambulances close to the field—and leave the engines running.

But if the flesh wasn't willing, the spirit was. That quality which had lifted these players above their peers when they were young—that competitive fire, the urge to excel—remained vibrantly alive, though their waists were thicker and legs heavier. Sure, the lot of them had come to D.C. to take advantage of the freebies, get in on a nice, long weekend with someone else picking up the tab. Bring the wife, see the sights. See some old friends. With the pressure off, a man like Roger Maris could relax and unwind with reporters, something he never did as a player. And ballplayers from one generation, like Enos Slaughter and Bob Feller, found they had more in common with the modern players, guys like Killebrew and Al Kaline, than they had previously thought. So it was a gathering place, but it developed into something more than that. These men hadn't come all that way to make fools of themselves, to have people laugh at them. They had too much pride for that.

Pee Wee Reese told a reporter, "You know you can't do anything anymore, and everybody else knows it. They [the fans] are saying, 'Look at this old goat.' But you still say to yourself, 'I'm gonna show these people what I can do.'" And the old-timers did exactly that. Richie Ashburn, age fifty-four, tried a drag bunt to get on base and start a rally. Fifty-nine-year-old Al Dark, playing shortstop, bluffed runners into sliding. "You always have your pride, which makes you play as hard as you can," said forty-three-year-old Willie McCovey, who hit a four-hundred-thirty-foot home run in batting practice. Camilo Pascual, a fit forty-seven, was the most impressive pitcher in the game, throwing very hard in his time on the mound.

Next to Al Rosen muffing an easy pop-up at third, the most embarrassing moment of the evening came when a fly ball smacked a beefy Henry Aaron in the chin in right field. But the forty-seven-year-old redeemed himself with a major league catch of a stinging line drive by Bill Freehan, robbing him of extra bases. "We're not playing to embarrass ourselves," Aaron said after the game. "We wanted to win."

If there were any doubts in Luke Appling's mind about the competitive nature of the event, the game's first pitch, a curveball, erased them. Befitting his status as the oldest man on the field, the seventy-five-year-old was given the honor of leading off for the American League. Opposing him was Warren Spahn, age sixty. It was agreed beforehand that curves would not be thrown during the game, but Spahn, a ferocious competitor who won a Purple Heart for bravery in

World War II, broke the rule on the very first pitch.

Throwing a curve was partly fun, kind of an impish joke. But it had a serious purpose too. With Al Kaline, forty-six, and Brooks Robinson, forty-four, coming up in the order, Spahn didn't want an old pushover like Appling getting on base. So he did what every good pitcher should do; he tried to cross the hitter up, get him off stride.

Opening with a curveball may have been a mistake, however. The pitch sent a message to Appling, who must have understood what it meant. This was baseball, *the real thing,* and let's see what you can do, old man. Luke stepped out of the batter's box to take a couple more swings. Then he stepped back in, waiting expectantly for what the crafty old left-hander would offer next.

In came the pitch. The pitcher followed through in a semblance of his youthful form and the batter reacted with an aggressiveness that had not entirely been extinguished by time. The drama of it was that nobody expected it. It was an astonishingly marvelous and surprising act. Spahn pitched and Appling swung and the ball, as John Updike wrote of a Ted Williams home run, "was in the books while it was still in the sky." It landed twelve rows deep in the short left field bleachers—a home run.

After the ball flew out of the park Spahn chased Appling around the bases slapping him good-naturedly with his glove. When Luke made it to the dugout, he clutched his heart and collapsed in the arms of his laughing teammates. In the locker room afterward he posed for photographers flexing his muscles. Reporters crowded around him, and he lit a cigar and told jokes like George Burns. Warren Spahn entered the room and came over to congratulate Appling, explaining, "I remember he hit the ball to the opposite field, so I thought I'd pitch him inside." Unfortunately, Spahn continued, he got the ball out over the plate with not much on it. Appling, overhearing this, quickly jumped in: "That's not true. It was a vicious curveball right on the fists," he said with a broad smile, adding, "Lemme tell you, Spahn. If you'd been in the American League when I played, I might have had another twelve or fifteen points on my batting average."

Appling's most famous hit was not a tremendous blow by major league standards, landing some two hundred fifty feet from home plate. But nobody in RFK Stadium seemed to care about that. The people in the stands jumped to their feet and shouted as the ball took off and then, as Spahn chased the hero of the day around the bases, they laughed and yelled with a childlike glee. The home run came to them as a gift. Appling had given them something—or, more precisely, something had been given to them all, including Appling.

Down on the field, Luke Appling trotted past Red Schoendienst and Pee Wee Reese. Willie Mays broke into a smile in center, Ernie Banks was thinking how great this was for everybody. Out of the American League dugout spilled Appling's teammates, Bob Feller, Whitey Ford, Johnny Mize, Early Wynn, coming to congratulate him. Luke ran the bases like an eleven-year-old after his first Little League home run. He was on air. Old Aches and Pains, for the moment, had none.

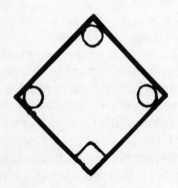

Acknowledgments

L IKE BLANCHE DUBOIS, I depended on the kindness of strangers to gather the material for this book. My research included books, magazines and newspaper articles too numerous to list here. but some specific works and authors deserve mention.

My understanding of Babe Ruth and his contribution to the game was greatly enriched by Robert Creamer's *Babe,* the best of the books about Ruth and one of the best baseball biographies ever done. I owe a debt to Charles Einstein not only for his fine biography of Willie Mays, *Willie's Time,* but for the personal kindness he showed me when I was working on my first book. *The Baseball Reader,* which features selections from The Fireside Books of Baseball, edited by Einstein, also provided information and inspiration. Lawrence Ritter's *The Glory of Their Times* is required reading for anyone interested in the game's early days, as are *Baseball When the Grass Was Real* and *The October Heroes,* two in the fine series of oral histories by Donald Honig.

Probably the best all-around baseball book published in the last ten years is *The Ultimate Baseball Book,* edited by Daniel Okrent and Harris Lewine, which continues to offer surprises and nuggets of lore after many nights of browsing through it. For the chapter on the Brooklyn Dodgers, Peter Golenbock's *Bums* and Roger Kahn's *The Boys of Summer* served as the bedrock for my understanding of the appeal of the team. Gay Talese's 1966 *Esquire* magazine article on Joe DiMaggio is as remarkable for its writing as its insights into its subject. To refresh my memory about baseball events of more recent vintage, I turned to Roger Angell's superb *Five Seasons,* a collection of his writings from *The New Yorker.*

My chronology of Billy Martin's greatest fights depended on several newspaper compilations, the most thorough of which was done by Lewis Leader of the *San Francisco Examiner.* My reconstruction of Luke Appling's greatest moment came after a close study of the reporting of the *Washington Post* sports staff, which was uniformly excellent. *How Life Imitates the World Series,* by the *Post*'s Tom Boswell, was lucid and entertaining and a rich source of anecdotes. Wherever one dips into *Strawberries in the Summertime* or *The Red Smith Reader,* two collections of columns by Red Smith, one finds wisdom and shimmering language that every writer of sports can only envy.

I drew upon the work of many other writers for this volume. They included: Lee Allen, Ron Fimrite, Roy Blount, Jr., Bob Chieger, Rich Marazzi, Len Fiorito, Jimmy Breslin, Bruce Jenkins, Lowell Cohn, Robert Peterson, Richard Donovan, Al Stump, Glenn Dickey, Harvey Frommer, Ed Linn, Maury Allen, Larry Merchant, Peter Gammons, Stan Isle, Scott Ostler. *The Baseball Encyclopedia* was of course an indispensable research tool, buttressed by *The Baseball Register* and *Daguerreotypes* published by The Sporting News.

Other people gave generously of their time and considerable expertise to offer opinions and editorial guidance. Robert Creamer, Charlie Singer, Peter Damm, Scott Thomason, Walt Daley and Bob Stevens all were kind enough to review parts of the manuscript and suggest improvements. David Nelson read a sizable portion of the text, and his comments and editorial advice were of incalculable benefit to me.

A week before deadline, when my Smith-Corona broke down, Max Lateiner lent me his company's office typewriter. When Max's company's typewriter broke down, I rented another from an office equipment store. I want to thank them both.

I also want to thank my wife Sheila, who did the illustrations for the book. In addition, she offered suggestions, listened patiently, and put up with me stewing over details in the middle of the night. Finally, my editor at Perigee, Gene Brissie, greatly encouraged and supported me, believing in the project and in my ability to do it. I hope his confidence was not misplaced.

KEVIN NELSON

Index